THE JACK RUSSELL TERRIER

Courageous Companion

CATHERINE ROMAINE BROWN

HOWELL BOOK HOUSE

NEW YORK

Howell Book House
A Simon & Schuster Macmillan Company
1633 Broadway
New York, NY 10019-6785

Macmillan Publishing books may be purchased for business or sales promotional use. For information please write: Special Markets Department, Macmillan Publishing USA, 1633 Broadway, New York, NY 10019-6785.

MACMILLAN is a registered trademark of Macmillan, Inc.
Library of Congress Cataloging-in-Publication

Brown, Catherine Romaine
The Jack Russell terrier: courageous companion / Catherine Romaine Brown.
   p. cm.
   Includes bibliographical references (p. 171) and index.
   ISBN 0-87605-195-6
   1. Jack Russell terrier. I. Title.
SF429.J27B764 1999
636.755—dc21   98-11631
                                      CIP

Manufactured in the United States of America
10 9 8 7 6 5

Cover and book design by George J. McKeon

Dedication

This book is dedicated to Nester Acorn of Treetop. Nester started my love for Jack Russell Terriers.

Contents

Foreword

*T*he times they are a changing. . . . nothing could be more true for the Jack Russell Terrier. This unique little working terrier, once known and loved only by the working terrier men of England, has now gained enormous notoriety. Jack Russells are now known throughout the world, and desired by many. They can be found in TV shows, movies, commercials and magazine ads; there seems to be no end to their versatility. Although they are now known *of* by many, they are known *well* only by those who have lived with and loved them for many years.

Long-time breed enthusiasts do not see this trend in popularity as an asset to this feisty little type of working terrier, but rather a possible threat to its future. Life with a Jack Russell Terrier is unique and, at times, trying—it is not for the weak of heart, the professional with little time at home or one who enjoys a sedentary lifestyle. It is only for those with a love of adventure and continuous activity, a strong will, a good sense of humor and the ability to understand and appreciate what is perhaps the most intelligent canine in the world.

Very little has been accurately written about the Jack Russell Terrier over the years, and there was little need for solid information until recently. People generally learned about Jack Russells only by meeting one or more and their owners, often around horse barns or sporting events. However, with Jack Russells seeming to appear just about everywhere, it is now very important that anyone attracted to this unique little dog have the opportunity to learn as much as possible before embarking on the adventure of owning one.

What is so unusual about Jack Russell Terriers? One might say it is their extreme intelligence, their unwavering courage, their enormous heart, their never-ending humorous antics, their amazingly athletic and energetic structure or their loyal devotion. If you can imagine an overabundance of all of these outstanding characteristics packed into a twelve- to fifteen-pound structure, with a body and brain that rarely slow down, you might begin to understand that this is no ordinary little dog.

Above all, one must remember that into this little dog was born a purpose: to work in the earth, sometimes as deep as fifteen feet or more below the surface, to locate and face a quarry equal or larger in size and strength and to drive it from the earth and on the run, so the hunt could go on. This was a big career for a little dog, requiring courage that is neither known nor understood by most canines or humans. Jack Russells are driven by pure instinct and love for their job.

Although not many Jack Russells in the United States today will do any real earth work, those who choose this type of companion must understand that it remains the soul of their existence. To know and appreciate this terrier is to understand what it is about. Digging is the function into which these terriers were born, and the instinct to perform this function has been preserved in this unique little working dog for nearly 200 years. To lose that drive and instinct, or to change the structure needed to fulfill the task, would be to turn this terrier into something else entirely.

Jack Russell Terriers can and do make wonderful pets and companions, in the right situation. However, their great intelligence and endless energy must be employed in some way, and safely channeled for the protection of the terrier and those around it. If this can be achieved, great harmony will abound, and you will enter an adventure that you will never want to be without till the day you die: life with a Jack Russell Terrier.

In this book you will learn a great deal about this little dog. Catherine Brown has years of experience with the working Jack Russell. She has dedicated many years to Russell Rescue, and her experiences with the rehabilitation of displaced Jack Russells will benefit everyone considering, or learning to live with, a Jack Russell Terrier. Read it carefully, and learn from its contents.

You may determine that this is not the dog for you. If so, you have probably made a thoughtful decision. If you choose to share your life with a Jack Russell Terrier, learn to understand the nature of the terrier, and protect its heritage and its future. Work with those who have preserved this unique dog for so many years, keeping it sound in mind and body. Its future lies in our hands. We hope we are up to the challenge.

TERRI BATZER
Administrator, Jack Russell Terrier Club of America

Acknowledgments

Ailsa Crawford, the founder of the Jack Russell Terrier Club of America, receives my deepest thanks for her tireless work creating the club and its excellent registry. She has done the most in her work to preserve, protect and encourage the work of this dog in the United States. Her dedication is an inspiration. My deepest admiration and respect are for her work on behalf of this terrier.

My appreciation for the dog directed me to dedication to the Jack Russell Terrier Club of America. The motto of the club, "Preserve, Protect, and Work the Jack Russell Terrier," covers much of what one needs to understand about the dog.

Terri Batzer deserves a stand-up ovation for her work for the Jack Russell and the JRTCA. It is not an easy job she has taken on behalf of this very popular dog. She steered me to my first book, *The Jack Russell Terrier: An Owner's Guide to a Happy, Healthy Pet*. Terri offers her time and heart to the breed and the club beyond the call of duty. She is a remarkable woman and has more energy than anyone I have ever met, even more than a Jack Russell Terrier.

Romaine J. Doran taught me both compassion and courage. The Jack Russell is a dog she would have loved. I wish to give memory and appreciation to Rushmore and Marion Mariner, who gave me my first two terriers. A special memorial to William Yull, who loved the little dogs, and Teresa Phillips, who would have been an excellent veterinarian.

I wish to thank Anthony Brown, who, for a good amount of years, took on life cheerfully with Jack Russell Terriers. He helped me tend, birth and train dogs. He dug in the dark and cold rain to recover a stubborn dog at work. He has helped me bury dogs I love. Tony had his trials relating to my dogs and my obsession with them. In hopelessness he declared the truth, "Catherine has gone to the dogs."

I also wish to thank my adult children, Peter Hraber III, who helped me with the understanding of genetics and computers, and Elizabeth Hraber, who has an uncanny way of presenting a fresh viewpoint to any situation. Both children are my teachers and dearest friends, and encouraged this project.

A tribute to the working terrier men of Great Britain must be included here. They are the lads who shaped the dog and kept it what it is, the remarkable working terrier.

Introduction

I must begin this project with a label of caution. Jack Russell Terriers are not the dog for everyone. If you invite one into your life, the relationship will be a little like that between a parent and a child. In fact, the intensity of the human–Jack Russell relationship has even been compared to a troubled romance. Living with a Jack Russell requires commitment.

The intelligence of the dog is without question. This is a breed that has been shaped by work, and the dog's desire and ability to work continues to direct its development. The Jack Russell is made of true grit. Although adorable in appearance, these dogs can be little thugs in white clown costumes.

Unfortunately, too many Jack Russell Terriers need new homes because their owners did not know they had invited a prey-focused hunting dog into their sedentary lives. You must know your life will never be quite the same again if you become the owner of one of these remarkable dogs. Do not purchase or adopt one until you fully understand what they need to be happy and safe. You must provide for their demanding requirements in order to have a successful, rewarding life with a Jack Russell Terrier, and it with you.

The Jack Russell Terrier: Is It the Right Breed for You?

Life with a Jack Russell changes things forever. The journey toward loving this dog may find the owner asking, "What have I gotten myself into?" Entering your life is a companion that wants and needs a purpose and a job. The Jack Russell is a dog with an enormous, fearless heart. Your heart will be stolen, and from time to time broken, by allowing a Jack Russell in.

CHARACTERISTICS OF THE JACK RUSSELL TERRIER

Jack Russells demand constant attention and stray if not attended to.

If they can't find trouble, they will make it.

Expect a whole lot of action.

The Jack Russell's history as a fox hunter shapes its desires, its behavior and its physique.

Never trust them alone outdoors for even a few minutes.

The JRT is not always easy to control.

Rest is brief.

Everything about the dog relates to its history as a fox-hunting terrier.

Loyalty or even attention to you can be replaced with the distraction on the horizon of a mouse or a leaf, to which the dog will run at full speed.

Expect the dog to ignore you, no matter how good a dog trainer you think you are!

If your dog's "recall" seems unbelievable, it probably is. Don't depend on your voice for control, ever.

JRTs can charm the skin off a snake and break your heart. They can snuggle with you one minute then dash off like they never knew you.

Expect surprises, both good and bad.

Housetraining is a state of mind more than a state of affairs. It can be political.

Dog spelled backwards makes some people uncomfortable, not Jack Russells.

Jack Russells like to take command of all they survey.

If you lack a sense of humor, this is not the dog for you.

Know what it is that your dog was bred to do, so you can determine if these traits are agreeable in your relationship. If allowed to be very good at something, a dog will be a nearly constant delight to you. Performing the functions for which it was bred is *everything* to the Jack Russell. Know what your dog's needs are and be sure you can provide them. Are you ready to deal with a high level of energy and enjoy it? Know the limitations of the dog and your relationship to it, if any. Know what and how much the dog has to do to be happy. The dog's behavior and yours are very closely linked, so you had better be sure this is a dog you can like for being itself. If dog hair or hogging the bed bothers you, rethink getting a JRT.

It must be understood that only the size of the dog is small: the Jack Russell has needs that rival those of any big dog. Everything else about the Jack Russell Terrier is larger than life. Do not select this dog for its size alone. Its personality is a major consideration in the selection process. You must be able to provide for the physical needs and the mental demands of this "enormous" little dog.

If you don't have a sense of humor, you won't really appreciate a JRT. (photo by Ken Hollis)

Jack Russell Terriers are handsome, hardy little dogs. They are compact and athletic. Some owners comment favorably on the olfactory level, stating that the dog even smells good!

By the Standards of the Jack Russell Terrier Club of America, Great Britain and its affiliates, the dog must range in size from ten to fifteen inches tall at the withers (the points of the scapula at the base of the neck). It must be at least 51 percent white in color. The markings may be brown, tan or black or combined. No brindle marking is permitted, as it indicates an infusion of another breed. It is important to know that the Jack Russell Terrier is a "strain" of terrier and not a "purebred."

A typical JRT is always waiting for something to happen, and if it can't find anything going on, it will create a diversion. Jack Russells want play and exercise, and in truth, there is no living with them if they do not get both. Rarely do they seem as if they have received enough of either. A Jack Russell Terrier will bounce back and want to continue to play or work long after its owner is exhausted.

The little Jack Russell delights at being on its toes and ready to go with its owner anywhere it may be allowed. Most love travel and feel obliged to guard the car, house or yard like a lion. Most, moreover, act as though they weighed in tenfold of their diminutive size. Whatever the situation, a Jack Russell wants to be the boss.

Jack Russells often pick a favorite person to whom they attach their affections and loyalty. They may be polite and affectionate to others, but they'll watch every move of the human they love most, following that beloved person from room to room, not unlike a shadow. Many dogs feel insulted to be

If you let a Jack Russell come along, you can bet it will be eager to do so!

"closed out"—even of the bathroom. It can be fairly said that they are possessive of those they love, often they very much want companionship with a particular human.

The appeal of Jack Russells is irresistible. Not only are they downright cute, one is struck with the intensity of their appearance. The dark-colored eyes radiate both humor and a marked intelligence—an intelligence that captivates those that look into them. They can be spellbinding. The Jack Russell's mind, like its body, is very busy!

HOW I FELL FOR THE JACK RUSSELL

I was never much of a dog fancier until the late Rushmore Mariner of Little Acorn Farm gave me Elbert Acorn. Rushmore raised horses and was a fox-hunting friend. Elbert was the essence of the Jack Russell Terrier except that he was large in the chest, which made it difficult for him to hunt below ground, as much as he wanted to. He was a beloved companion that liked to play ball when work was to be done.

If you get selected as the dog's favorite human, be prepared to be followed around—constantly.

On the farm, the men would dig holes to put in fence posts. Elbert would drop his tennis ball in the freshly dug fragrant earth and bark until a worker would retrieve it. If no ball was available, he would find a rock for his play. You could throw the rock in the pond and Elbert would dive underwater and retrieve—often the same rock. It was endless, compulsive play. When we thought about getting a second dog so that Elbert would have someone to play with in addition to his human family, the Mariners gave me Nester Acorn, a lovely dog that was small in size but big in spirit.

When Elbert and Nester first met, they would hunt together on the farm. I could be mowing the lawn and Elbert would come to me with dirt on his face and paws, all excited for me to follow where Nester was deep in the ground baying at a groundhog in the horse pasture. Elbert was the scout and messenger. I would have to stop whatever I was doing and get the shovel and dig to Nester. There was no calling

The Jack Russell would not be considered by most to be a pensive dog—nonetheless, it is always thinking.

him out. I had no interest in anything living in the ground, or in a dog's relationship to these animals in holes. This was, however, my introduction to hunting with terriers—forever directing my life to the dedication of these wonderful, complicated, intelligent little hunting dogs.

I soon learned that having two male dogs was not the right combination for harmony. Before long, the two squared off, intending to fight to the finish. Keeping both dogs was out of the question, and Elbert went to live with our farrier, Ron Forbes.

With Nester still in the home, I became interested in terrier activities. He won many go-to-ground competitions at Jack Russell Terrier Club of America and American Working Terrier Association sanctioned trials and earned the JRTCA Bronze Medallion for honor in the field hunting. He slept in my bed at night and was my best dog friend.

One time, on a simple walk in the woods with friends, Nester went into a den he encountered with his mate, Bolt 'Em Kodi. The dogs would not come out, and it was getting dark and cold. I would not leave the dogs, which were silent and only whimpered from time to time when I called to them. Another friend had been called for help. By midnight, we had a crew cutting down trees and coming with a back hoe, and we were able to rescue both dogs. A mangy fox had blocked their exit. Without the back hoe and true friends, both dogs would have been lost. Nester could never be trusted to come when called if he found a fox den. He had become headstrong and foolish in his mission to meet foxes.

The call of the wild was more than he could bear. He vanished in his favorite fox den on our farm in March 1995 and could not be found again, even with help from friends from neighboring states and Canada. A heroic dig was attempted without recovery. As Mike Kelley, an equine reporter, stated about Nester's passing, "He died with his boots on." It was a noble but senseless death. It was part of the courting of sorrow in loving this brave dog, filled with abandon and focus. Nester made his mark on me forever.

Prior to Nester's demise, Dru Malavase would bring his grandsire over and we would hunt groundhogs out of the horse pastures together. The large holes made by groundhogs are notable sources of leg-breaking falls for horses. We learned from the dogs and enjoyed their instincts at work. We were housewives that had fun with our dogs. Soon farmers began asking that we bring the dogs to locate and reduce the pests from fields and orchards. In the evening when the chickens roosted, we were welcome in henhouses to reduce the rat population.

Following foxes on horseback with hounds has been an interest and activity of mine for several years. The link of the Jack Russell and working packs of foxhounds was a tradition for many years, but this link was recently broken in the United States. After footage of terriers pitching into a fox

Jack Russells are courageous to a fault, and there are many stories of their heroics.

was televised in the United Kingdom and the United States, the Master of Foxhounds Association changed its policy, ceasing terrier work in connection with any recognized pack of foxhounds. The film fanned the anti-hunting fires with unbridled harshness, and with blame to the terrier. It is my most sincere hope that application of terrier work with foxhounds will be restored in the United States.

It is not the harvest of the fox that attracts followers. The fox is a beautiful and intelligent animal worthy of study and praise. However, it is considered a nuisance in many lands where it kills spring lambs, chickens and other fowl. In the United States one is thrilled to catch even a glimpse of a red fox. Historically, the terrier is a locator and below-ground bolter of foxes rather than a dispatcher.

Terriers are rarely used for helping man to provide a food source. Some have been trained to work birds or rabbits, but most are used for vermin control. Terriers have a deep history of working along with foxhounds for bolting earthed foxes put to ground. Dogs have been used for pest control and work in any hunting capacity when they are of the inclination and mettle to do so. This history

The JRT excels at locating the fox, but it was not bred to harm its quarry.

notable success as a locator of quarry for its handler. Here is a dog that is willing to go deep into earthen dens to locate and bay at the fox, without physical combat, for hours and even days. When at work, Jack Russells have been known to stay in earths for two weeks without food or water.

Nester Acorn had taken me to uncharted territory from which I was not to return. Before long, I became acquainted with and joined the Jack Russell Terrier Club of America (JRTCA). My involvement with the dog and club became a passion. The club is full of JRT enthusiasts and teaches others about the dog. My first volunteer job was as a state representative for the club; later I apprenticed and became a working judge and a conformation judge.

of function is retained by both selective breeding and training of the dogs inclined to work.

It would be a sad ending to the chapter on human history to condemn fox hunting, which is more accurately fox chasing. Keep in mind the people that relate in the hunting field to quarry are the staunch supporters of keeping the animals in the wild plentiful and healthy. They will contribute to the aid of wildlife in an earnest, supportive way.

Every aspect of the makeup of the Jack Russell Terrier reflects the qualities and attributes of the red fox. The dog that is put together correctly can move freely and be swift above and below ground. The intelligence of the dog contributes to its

The Jack Russell that is well put together can move freely—it is swift above ground and determined below.

Your companionship is one of the greatest gifts to a Jack Russell.

Fate would have it that the JRTCA Russell Rescue became necessary. As a board member of the club in 1991, I took on the task of setting up a system of placement service for lost and misunderstood dogs in transition. I was inspired by the death of a dog that I had sold. Sadly, the dog was killed before I could find him a home where he could live and hunt safely with supervision. Hundreds of dogs have been placed in permanent, suitable homes as a result of the organization's efforts.

WHAT YOU SEE MIGHT NOT BE WHAT YOU GET

I cannot overemphasize the demands of being the human counterpart to this little dog. If you think you are getting a well-behaved and clever dog filled with polite tricks, you are in for a rude awakening. The JRTs you see on television and in movies are exceedingly well-trained dogs that, on-screen, are working with highly experienced trainers. Off-screen they act exactly like their contemporaries. Those who work with Jack Russells for films and television know how willful they can be. All Jack Russells have very strong personalities.

The perfectly trained JRT will chase a cat or take off to seek activity at the drop of a hat. If the mood strikes, your dog may choose to completely ignore you. Unfortunately, people see the clever side of the breed and base their decision to purchase one on that basis, without realizing how spirited a clever dog can be. What they are seeing is clearly not what the dog is. One of the most difficult tricks to teach a Jack Russell is to stay still.

While a fair number of Jack Russells find work in the entertainment industry, one could argue that they best like to entertain themselves.

Finally, the dogs need their bodies and minds exercised in order to be balanced and happy. If your lifestyle requires you to be gone many hours a day, don't frustrate a JRT by making it wait long hours for human companionship. This is a dog that desires your company and to simply be near you. If you come home tired and don't consistently want to give exercise or play to a dog that will delight in your arrival, don't get a Jack Russell Terrier. A Jack Russell loves a daily routine and will look forward to its intense play and exercise on a very regular basis. This is a dog that needs an owner who is willing to participate in activity and to devote sufficient time to providing it with companionship. The Jack Russell has been kept as more than a pet; it has been kept as a working dog with a job. This is a dog that must have a purpose and an outlet for its intelligence and energy to be happy.

CHAPTER 2

A Brief History of the Jack Russell Terrier

The history of the Jack Russell Terrier is much more than the history of one man. Although the legend of Parson John Russell (1795–1883) has gone far to popularize the working strain of the Fox Terrier, many men of the British Isles had been working on the strain of small, white-bodied working Fox Terriers for a century before. It is vital to the complete understanding of these dogs to know that they were not originally bred to be pets.

The dog was created to hunt vermin below ground. Knowing the heritage of this worker makes one better understand the total picture of the dog. Many of the perceived "problems" associated today with the JRT arise because it has always been (and one hopes will remain) willing to work.

In an article titled the "Working Terrier Past and Present" written for Blackwood's *Edinburgh Magazine* (New York, October 1907), T. F. Dale wrote:

The man who loves hounds is sure to be interested in terriers. The foxhound and the terrier are connected in our minds by their common enmity to the fox. Indeed, in the warfare against the fox the terrier has been an ally of man for a much longer period then the hound. When stag-hunting was the sport of kings, and before the idea of the fox as a beast of chase had dawned on the nobles and gentry in England and Scotland, the peasants and the terriers were harrying the

This little white-bodied dog was not originally bred to serve as a pet.

fox even in his stronghold of Malepartus, as they do to his day in Scotland or Wales, and in the mountain districts of Westmoreland and Cumberland.

It was no doubt in their warfare against vermin that the terriers acquired the characteristics of gameness, hardihood, and intelligence which their successors have inherited. Their evolution has followed the same course as that of all modern breeds of sporting dogs. Chosen at first for working qualities only, it is later refinement which has grafted beauty on to ability. The division of terriers into breeds and their classification at dog shows is quite a modern development. Terrier was a name given to any hardy, active little dog that would face a badger or a fox in its earth, or sometimes a cat in a corner, the last named being by no means the least formidable antagonist of the three....

There was no exclusiveness in the breeding of a terrier, and he was crossed with the bull-dog to give him

courage, with the beagle to improve his nose, and in later days the greyhound to give him speed. The crossing was limited only by the necessities of his work, for the terrier needed to be a comparatively small dog, since a dog over sixteen pounds is too large and below twelve pounds too small to be of use for going to ground. I know of course that weight has more to do with make and muscular development than with size, yet nevertheless the weights give a rough method of estimating the limits of serviceable size for the working terrier.

THE LEGACY OF PARSON JOHN RUSSELL

Parson John Russell lived from 1795 to 1883 in England and, according to legend, developed one of the finest strains of Fox Terriers for working fox in Devonshire, England. Apart from his church activities he was known as a man passionate for the sport of fox hunting and the breeding of fox-hunting dogs. It has been said he was a colorful and flamboyant character. John Russell was well known throughout England. His funeral was well attended, as he was a legendary figure of his times in the sporting community. His enormous personality may account for the fact that a working strain of Fox Terrier carries his name.

The popularity of Fox Terriers reached its zenith in the late 1800s. The breed was accepted as a Kennel Club breed and underwent many conformational changes at the whim of the show ring. (The Kennel Club is the United Kingdom's leading registry governing body of purebred dogdom, as the American Kennel Club is here in the United

States.) It was not long before the Fox Terrier had an upright scapula and a deepened chest. Even the head of the Fox Terrier lengthened and narrowed in style. Show Fox Terriers, by structure, could not enter a shallow earth even if the instinct to do so remained. They no longer were akin to the Fox Terriers at work in hunt kennels or dear to men who sought a bit of hunting while away from labor.

As the popular Fox Terrier went to the bench shows, Parson John Russell and the working terrier men went into the fields and followed hounds in pursuit of foxes. John Russell was one of the original founders of England's Kennel Club in 1873. In 1874 he judged Fox Terriers in the first Kennel Club–sanctioned show in England. He remained a member of the club but did not exhibit his own dogs. As John Russell described his dogs: "True terriers they were, but differing from the present show dogs as the wild eglantine differs from a garden rose."

Parson John Russell was a flamboyant character with a passion for hunting.

The show Fox Terrier was favored wearing a smooth coat. John Russell bred the less popular wire-haired terriers (now termed rough- or broken-coated). The heavier coats were more suitable for hunting dogs. John Russell said of the Fox Terrier, "A real Fox Terrier is not meant to murder and his intelligence should always keep him from such a crime." Because the terrier ran with hounds and put in a hard day's work, good stamina and tenacity were needed. Often the terrier had to cut corners or catch up with hounds, or even anticipate where the chase might end to do its job. This was the blood of the old type of Fox Terrier, not those of the show ring.

John Russell's foundation bitch was one named Trump, whom he bought from a milkman in the Oxfordshire village of Marten while still an undergraduate student at Oxford University in 1819. Trump was the ideal terrier in Russell's eyes. A painting of the dog still hangs in the harness room at Sandringham Castle in Norfolk, England. She was white with a patch

Trump, John Russell's foundation bitch, was purchased from a milkman.

of dark tan over each eye and ear, with a similar dot not larger than a British penny at the base of her tail. Her coat was reportedly thick, close and wiry but not the long jacket of the Scottish Terrier. Her legs were as straight as arrows and her feet were perfect. Russell said of Trump, "Her whole appearance gave indications of courage, endurance, and hardihood. Her size has been compared to a full grown vixen fox."

Reverend John Russell's circle of friends included the Prince of Wales, King Edward VII and others who were also Masters of Foxhounds. Late in life, he would continue to hack long distances to attend meets. Russell became the vicar of Swymbridge in 1832. He was occupied by both his church duties and those of being a Master of Foxhounds. Legend has it the bishop of his diocese

once accused Russell of refusing to bury a child's body on a Wednesday because it interfered with the hunt. There are stories of the bishop asking Russell repeatedly to give up his hounds and hunting. He tactfully agreed to give up his hounds, saying, "Mrs. Russell shall keep them."

In England the red fox is considered vermin, a killer of spring lambs and poultry. The hunt helped control the balance of domesticated animals and wild ones wastefully feeding on the farmer's stock. By request of the farmer, a hunt could be summoned to a farm for control of a persistent menacing fox, and it was considered appropriate to dispose of foxes encountered during the hunt if the farmer so desired.

Today's hunts are not all bad news for foxes. In fact, foxes seem to exhibit a sense of humor about the hounds singing to their scent or being at a safe distance. Sometimes they will perch and watch calmly as the pack draws nearer. They remain unruffled. The fox is very intelligent and knows its territory. The pleasure this country sport affords those of all ages is the enjoyment of the sights and sounds of good hound work. When fair terrier work is possible with a noncombative terrier employed, one can well understand John Russell's fondness for the chase. He was reportedly not interested in the killing of foxes. Russell participated in the chase well into his late eighties.

Upon John Russell's death at eighty-eight years of age, his stock was scattered. What does live

The hardy little terrier popularized by Parson John Russell lives on—more popular than ever!

on is his type or strain of hardy, old-fashioned willing-to-work terrier. Those who did not hunt were culled along the way or were kept as pets in homes of nonsporting people. Some that did not conform correctly for earth work or had too much blood of other breeds were kept by stable owners that used the terriers above ground for the task of rodent control.

The ancient original strains of Fox Terriers were based on white terriers now extinct. Many British hunt kennels kept their own local strains of terriers used with their hounds. In England many a man lacking wealth or a fine horse would keep a few terriers. Working men would enjoy time away from their regular weekly jobs with sport with their own dogs. The ability of the dog to afford a man some sport locating fox or badger meant more than any pedigree that a dog might carry on

paper. One working dog was bred to another, and the strain remained strong in its instinct. The terrier was developed to use its nose and eyes to hunt.

THE DEVELOPMENT OF TODAY'S JACK RUSSELL TERRIER

Although the Reverend Parson left a legacy behind, the dog that bears his name is quite dissimilar to the dog that he bred. Greg Mousley, Chairman of the Jack Russell Terrier Club of Great Britain and the United World Terrier Federation, is a notable hunting man of Great Britain and a world authority on Jack Russell Terriers. Greg is a colorful, contemporary terrier-man. In his *History and Origin of the Jack Russell Terrier,* Mousley writes:

> To write accurately and knowledgeably on this subject we must first accept two things: first that history is a collection of facts and origin is purely speculation based on facts. We must find a base to begin, a point in time when fact takes over from probabilities and likelihood.
>
> The second thing we must get used to is the plain fact that the predominantly white terriers we have today known as "Jack Russells" owe nothing to the Devonshire sporting Parson other than his name.
>
> Many claim to have the blood of his terriers in their lines and in truth many "Modern Fox Terriers" can trace sparse links to terriers from his kennels. Whether he bred them or not is another matter and one which was much argued among Fox Terrier breeders around the turn of the century. However, as far as Jack

Noted authority Greg Mousley explaining the function and structure of the Jack Russell Terrier.

the status of the terrier. Indeed, until that time, the terrier had always been the forte of the working man, many of whom could neither read nor write and so memory served well enough and pedigrees were considered unnecessary.

The recently formed and none too popular "Parson Russell Club" supports the old fourteen-inch, fourteen-pound theory and too many are way above that. This rule of thumb comes from the practice of running terriers with hounds to assist hounds to draw thick and dense cover, particularly in the early part of the season before the frosts have helped to reduce and kill off thick cover. Parson Jack Russell was no exception. The thick gorse brakes he hunted still exist to this day. He used these larger, leggier terriers extensively with his hounds and they were seen out hunting on a regular basis.

Parson Jack Russell was an exuberant and eccentric character, often prone to exaggeration. Much was written about him by the old hunting scribes of the day and, along him, his terriers were mentioned too. Hence they became well known and, like all things, well talked of. Therefore, they became in demand and this prompted Russell in his later years to expand his kennel to meet a demand and, in order to do this, he gathered terriers from many sources.

In all likelihood he owed his fame in terriers to one or two good sorts. This is apparent when reading any article on this man. The same few names crop up every time. Indeed, how many self-styled experts of today owe their credibility to one or at best two good terriers? Sadly there are some who proclaim knowledge and expertise without owning even one well-known "Jack Russell"; let alone breeding one!

Russells are concerned, forget it. Their ancestry is far more complicated than that.

That Parson John Russell was a sporting man cannot be denied. His interest in hunting was developed at an early age. Terriers have for hundreds of years been synonymous with hounds so it is no surprise that he became interested in terriers. They were part and parcel of his hunting passion. Unfortunately, like many professional and amateur huntsmen of today, the terrier was regarded by most of the foxhunting hierarchy as a very poor relation of the hound. Hound pedigrees have been kept for many hundreds of years and hound breeding has been, and in some cases still is, the lifelong passion of hunting fanatics. Not so the humble terrier whose pedigrees were seldom kept. It was not until the fashionable explosion during the 1800s of the "Modern Fox Terrier" and its forerunners do we see a change in

The Jack Russell was named in tribute to Parson John Russell and in order to distinguish the breed from the Fox Terrier.

Back to the Parson. As stated previously, the Parson Russell was an extrovert and a flamboyant character and in his role as "the sporting Parson" he became very well known and, through the sporting press, his fame spread and with it came social invitations. Along with this fame went the awareness of his terriers and, when the Fox Terrier Club was formed, a name was needed for the many thousands of white-bodied working terriers belonging to the working terriermen of the day in order to distinguish them from their Kennel Club counterparts.

The name Jack Russell had long been associated with white working terriers by word of mouth, the sporting press, and by his own claims to fame. It is not difficult to accept that, in a short time, any predominantly white working terrier was dubbed "Jack Russell" in order to disassociate these noble workers from the victims of the Kennel Club fad and fancy brigade who had already left the working terrierman and gone their own ill-fated way.

Rest assured the terrier we have today was around a very long time before the Parson Jack Russell was born. The Midlands have always been the stronghold of the white working terrier. The early winners in Fox Terrier Classes during the mid-1800s all came from the Grove, the Oakley, the Quorn, the Belvoir and the Rufford, all Midland packs. It was to the Midlands that Parson Russell looked to improve his kennel. This is just another fact to prove that, no matter what may be fantasized by others, Parson Russell did not develop the terrier that bears his name.

So where did this terrier come from? Let us speculate a while. That the terrier had mixed ancestry is without doubt and there is also no doubt that the rough-coated, hard-bitten, black-and-tan terrier played a large part in its creation. Depending on where in the United Kingdom one happened to be, the greater or lesser the effect.

The Old English White played an important role in the make-up of our terrier, although he was a crossbreed. His influence would again vary depending on one's geographical location. It is safe to say, however, that prior to the Industrial Revolution, the terriers that were destined to be "refined and perfected," were a veritable foreign legion, a very mixed bunch which had been around for a long time. Along with the Industrial Revolution came a change of environment, particularly for the working man and, along with him, a change for man's best friend—his terrier.

From the industrial Midlands and the north of Great Britain came many well-known breeds. Most owe their existence and ancestry to the rat pits and the dog fighting fanatics of the day.

The overspill from these breedings leached out into the countryside and influenced the already strong lines of working terriers used by foxhounds, gamekeepers, ratmen and the working terrier enthusiasts.

As early as the mid-1700s many types had become well established and the dealers and breeders of the day became fanatical, and wherever sporting men gathered, it was not long before heated arguments took place as to the quality and attributes of one type or another, a trend which lasts to this day.

For the next 100 years or so, terriers enjoyed a gradual rise in popularity. From this point I am only going to talk of the type of terrier that has developed into the "Jack Russell" of today, the white-bodied working terrier. Around the mid-1800s something happened to change the working terrier world forever— "The Dog Show."

When dog shows first started in the 1860s any white terrier with markings or not was shown as a Fox Terrier. The Fox Terrier Club was formed and everyone set out enthusiastically to perfect the type. However, it soon became apparent to the working terrier man that the terrier was changing. The terrier that had earned its place in the hearts and kennels of the working terrier-man now found itself on the hearth rug of the rich and famous. The spirit, stamina, tenacity and character, the result of hundreds of years of development, was forfeited for mere points of conformation, many of which were becoming ever exaggerated by a committee of non-working terrier people.

Take a look at the Modern Fox Terrier and you will see that the suspicions of the working terrier man of over one hundred years ago were well-founded. They knew that, without the overriding "earthwork" factor, the dog would change.

The true terrier men soon left the ranks of the Kennel Club and went their own way. Thank God they had the courage and foresight to resist the temptation of the big money and pseudo fame.

That this terrier of ours had a mixed ancestry is obvious but, even when the various types of white working terriers were well-established, more mixing and matching took place. Bull Terrier blood was frequently used. Beagle was infused to produce a scent hunting terrier. Some rabbiting fanatics put in Whippet blood to produce a small, agile, hardy terrier that could catch rabbits. Every single terrier breed and sometimes non-terrier breeds were used by individuals to adapt this terrier to their particular needs.

All this mixed blood was overspilled into the vast genetic pool of the Jack Russell Terrier, adding hybrid vigor and an adaptability second to none.

It says much for the conscientious breeders of yesteryear that they could swallow up this drastic cross-breeding and produce at the end of the day a smart workmanlike terrier with a conformation to match his job and the courage, stamina and character to see it through.

Another factor greatly determined the development of the different types of white terrier and that was one of transport. I firmly believe that the different types that are still there to be seen today owe as much to the following as they do to the influences of other breeds.

That the working Jack Russell was the forte of the working man is fact. In the early days the working man had no transport other than his legs, the occasional loan of the pony and trap and, in later years, the bicycle. This restriction on transport meant that when a bitch came into season, the amount of good stud dogs available was limited, to say the least, and it follows that the best of a few were frequently used. In order to be the best in a given area, the terrier would have to be an expert in his work and very consistent. He would be, in short, the ideal working terrier for the local terrain. The better he was built for the job, the longer he lasted and the more influence he would have. He also had to be a good producer, stamping his type, in short genetically powerful.

Again, another factor in the case of the Midlands is that terrier men here could use studs from around the four points of the compass without too much travel. It has not been mere chance that the Midlands has long been considered the area that has influenced the Jack Russell Terrier the most. Nowhere else can such a vast difference in working conditions be encountered in such a relatively small area from the granite, gritstone and limestone of the North, down through the clay and gravel and on to the flint, sandstone and loam of the South Midlands.

The types that were developed many years ago, both genetically and geographically, are much diluted today due to modern travel but they are still there to be seen by the keen observer. This dilution of the local types

gave much to the terrier. It strengthened its inbuilt hybrid vigor and leveled out the variation to a great extent.

More recently, the Jack Russell has had to withstand many introductions of foreign blood. The Bull Terrier was again introduced by a few during the 1960s and the Lakeland Fell cross made itself very popular in the late 1980s. Luckily these latest trends have been short lived and already the more traditional types have absorbed the contamination and are generally none the worse. These short-cut measures are practiced by a few individuals who cannot take the time to produce the type of dog they require or fancy by using the already existing kennels of Jack Russells in the United Kingdom. They believe that if they produce one or two outstanding examples, it is well worth it, not caring a dot for the amount of wastage they produce.

It is neither necessary nor desirable to cross breed any further outside the existing Jack Russell bloodlines. It has all been done in the past. Breeders should take advantage of what has gone before and just take a little more time and trouble. Within the ranks of the Jack Russell Terrier can be found the dog of anyone's dreams. A more versatile animal will not be found nor created. The Jack Russell Terrier can and will fulfill any and all working situations and a more loyal companion will not be found anywhere. He is the most versatile animal in the dog world. He has been preserved for us by generations of working terrier men. Let us ensure that we preserve this dog for those yet to come.

★*"History and Origin of the Jack Russell Terrier" by Greg Mousley, March 1998. Reprinted with permission from the author.*

CHAPTER 3

The Official Breed Standard with Interpretation

The Jack Russell Terrier was admitted into the American Kennel Club's Miscellaneous Class on January 1, 1998. The Standard adopted by the American Kennel Club (AKC) is considered the Official Standard for the Jack Russell Terrier, and because most people are familiar with the AKC, this organization's Standard appears first. A less detailed Standard is employed by the Jack Russell Terrier Club of America and by its parent club, the Jack Russell Terrier Club of Great Britain. This second Standard, and a discussion thereof, follows the Official Standard set forth below.

OFFICIAL STANDARD FOR THE JACK RUSSELL TERRIER

GENERAL APPEARANCE—The Jack Russell Terrier was developed in the south of England in the 1800s as a white terrier to work European red fox both above and below ground. The terrier was named for Reverend John Russell, whose terriers trailed hounds and bolted foxes from dens so the hunt could ride on.

To function as a working terrier, he must possess certain characteristics: a ready attitude, alert and confident; balance in height and length; medium in size and bone, suggesting strength and endurance. Important to breed type is a natural appearance: harsh, weatherproof coat with a compact construction and clean silhouette. The coat is broken or smooth. He has a small, flexible chest to enable him to pursue quarry underground and sufficient length of leg to follow the hounds. Old scars and injuries, the result of honorable work or accident, should not be allowed to prejudice a terrier's chance in the show ring, unless they interfere with movement or utility for work or breeding.

SIZE, SUBSTANCE, PROPORTION

Size—Both sexes are properly balanced between 12 inches and 14 inches at the withers. The ideal height of a mature dog is 14 inches at the withers, and bitches 13 inches. Terriers whose heights measure either slightly larger or smaller than the ideal are not to be penalized in the show ring provided other points of their conformation, especially balance and chest span, are consistent with the breed standard. The weight of a terrier in hard working conditions is usually between 13 and 17 lbs. *Proportion*—Balance is the keystone of the terrier's anatomy. The chief points of consideration are the relative proportions of

Balance is the keystone of the terrier's anatomy.

skull and foreface, head and frame, height at withers and length of body. The height at withers is slightly greater than the distance from the withers to tail, i.e., by possibly one and a half inches on a 14-inch dog. The measurement will vary according to height, the ratio of height to back being approximately 6:5. *Substance*—The terrier is of medium bone, not so heavy as to appear course or so light as to appear racy. The conformation of the whole frame is indicative of strength and endurance.

Disqualification—Height under 12 inches or over 15 inches.

HEAD

Head—Strong and in good proportion to the rest of the body, so the appearance of balance is maintained. *Expression*—Keen, direct, full of life and intelligence. *Eyes*—Almond shaped, dark in color, moderate in size, not protruding. Dark rims are desirable. *Ears*—Button ear. Small "V"-shaped drop ears of moderate thickness, carried forward close to the head with the tip so as to cover the orifice and pointing toward the eye. Fold is level with the top of the skull or slightly above. When alert, ear tips do not extend below the corner of the eye. *Skull*—Flat and fairly broad between the ears, narrowing slightly to the eyes. The stop is well defined but not prominent. Muzzle: Length from nose to stop is slightly shorter than the distance from stop to occiput. *Jaws*—Upper and lower are of fair and punishing strength. *Nose*—Nose must be black and fully pigmented. *Bite*—Teeth are large with complete dentition in a perfect scissors bite, i.e., upper teeth closely overlapping the lower teeth and teeth set square to the jaws. *Faults*—Light or yellow eye, round eye. Hound ear, fleshy ear, rounded tips. Level bite, missing teeth. Overshot, undershot or wry mouth.

The JRT chest should be flexible and compressible.

NECK, TOPLINE, BODY

Neck—Clean and muscular, moderately arched, of fair length, gradually widening so as to blend well into the shoulders. *Topline*—Strong, straight and level in motion, the loin slightly arched. *Body*—In overall length to height proportion, the dog appears approximately square and balanced. The back is neither short nor long. The back gives no appearance of slackness but is laterally flexible, so that he may turn around in an earth. Tuck-up is moderate. *Chest*—Narrow and of moderate depth, giving an athletic rather than heavily chested appearance; must be flexible and compressible. The ribs are fairly well sprung, oval rather than round, not extending past the level of the elbow. *Tail*—Set high, strong, carried gaily but not over the back or curled. Docked to the tip is approximately level to the skull, providing a good

handhold. *Faults*—Chest not spannable or shallow, barrel ribs. Tail set low or carried low to or over the back, i.e., squirrel tail.

FOREQUARTERS

Shoulders—Long and sloping, well laid back, cleanly cut at the withers. Point of shoulder sits in a plane behind the point of the prosternum. The shoulder blade and upper arm are of approximately the same length; forelimbs are placed well under the dog. Elbows hang perpendicular to the body, working free of the sides. Legs are strong and straight with good bone. Joints turn neither in nor out. Pasterns firm and nearly straight. *Feet*—Round, cat-like, very compact, the pads thick and tough, the toes moderately arched pointing forward, turned neither in nor out. *Faults*—Hare feet.

HINDQUARTERS

Strong and muscular, smoothly molded, with good angulation and bend of stifle. Hocks near the ground, parallel, and driving in action. Feet as in front.

COAT

Smooth—Double-coated. Coarse and weatherproof. Flat but hard, dense and abundant, belly and undersides of thighs not bare.

Broken—Double-coated. Coarse and weatherproof. Short, dense undercoat covered with a harsh, straight, tight jacket which lies flat and close to the body and legs. There is a clear outline with only a hint of eyebrows and beard. Belly and undersides of thighs are not bare. Coat does not show a strong tendency to curl or wave. *No sculptured furnishings. The terrier is shown in his natural appearance not excessively groomed. Sculpturing to be severely penalized.* Faults—Soft, silky, woolly, or curly topcoat. Lacking undercoat.

A white coat, with markings confined to the head and the root of the tail, is preferred.

COLOR

White, white with black or tan markings, or a combination of these, tri-color. Colors are clear. Markings are preferably confined to the head and root of the tail. Heavy body markings are not desirable. Grizzle is acceptable and should not be confused with brindle.

Disqualification—Brindle markings.

GAIT—Movement or action is the crucial test of conformation. The terrier's movement is free, lively, well coordinated, with straight action in front and behind. There should be ample reach and drive with a good length of stride.

TEMPERAMENT— Bold and friendly. Athletic and clever. At work he is a game hunter, tenacious and courageous. At home he is playful, exuberant and overwhelmingly affectionate. He is an independent and energetic terrier and requires his due portion of attention. He should not be quarrelsome. Shyness should not be confused with submissiveness. Submissiveness is not a fault. *Sparring is not acceptable.* **FAULT**—shyness.

Disqualification—Overt aggression toward another dog or human.

The Jack Russell is a playful, exuberant dog. (photo by Michael Schreiber)

SPANNING

To measure a terrier's chest, span from behind, raising only the front feet from the ground, and compress gently. Directly behind the elbows is the smaller, firm part of the chest. The central part is usually larger but should feel rather elastic. Span with hands tightly behind the elbows on the forward portion of the chest. The chest must be easily spanned by average-size hands. Thumbs should meet at the spine and fingers should meet under the chest. *This is a significant factor and a critical part of the judging process. The dog cannot be correctly judged without this procedure.*

DISQUALIFICATIONS

Height under 12 inches or over 15 inches

Prick ears

Liver nose

Four or more missing teeth

Overshot, undershot or wry mouth

Brindle markings

Overt aggression toward other dogs or humans

EFFECTIVE JANUARY 1, 1998

JACK RUSSELL TERRIER CLUB OF AMERICA STANDARD

In contrast, the breed standard established by the Jack Russell Terrier Club of Great Britain and the Jack Russell Terrier Club of America and its affiliates, asks for the following traits and requirements.

CHARACTERISTICS: The terrier must present a lively, active and alert appearance. It should impress with its fearless and happy disposition. It should be remembered that the Jack Russell is a working terrier and should retain these instincts. Nervousness, cowardice or over-aggressiveness should be discouraged, and it should always appear confident.

The Jack Russell Terrier must be a ready-for-action terrier, on its toes every waking moment. It is a dog that radiates an impressive level of fearlessness. This dog has a happy, cheerful disposition and a smile on its face, so to speak. Although trigger-quick for action, it is not nervous or yappy. It should not be cowardly, nor demonstrate fearfulness by skulking or acting timid; the Jack Russell has been bred for courage.

The Jack Russell should not be aggressive in its relations with humans. The dog is meant to work with its handler, and in this capacity should be cheerful and willing. It must never be made to feel humiliated or encouraged to be overly aggressive.

The Jack Russell is a tough terrier, very much on its toes all the time.

GENERAL APPEARANCE: A sturdy, tough terrier, very much on its toes all the time, measuring between 10 inches and 15 inches at the withers. The body length must be in proportion to the height, and it should present a compact, balanced image, always being in solid, hard condition.

The five-inch variation between minimum and maximum heights may seem unusual, but the dogs produced under this broad standard provide their owners with the variety required to meet the owners' needs. Different types of quarry require different-sized dogs.

HEAD: The head should be well balanced and in proportion to the body. The skull should be flat, of moderate width at the ears, narrowing to the eyes. There should be a defined stop, but not overpronounced. The length of the muzzle from the nose to the stop should be slightly shorter than the distance from the stop to the occiput. The nose should be black. The jaw should be powerful and well boned with strongly muscled cheeks.

Unlike the Fox Terrier's head, the Jack Russell's head should have a defined yet not too severe stop. The head should be in harmony with body. A tiny, weak-looking head is not appropriate for a hunting dog, nor is a massive head that looks as though it could stop up an earthen tunnel or make the dog appear head-heavy.

EYES: The eyes should be almond shaped, dark in color and full of life and intelligence.

The Jack Russell likes to make and hold eye contact with people. In this gesture and in the alert, intelligent look

EXTERNAL FEATURES OF A JACK RUSSELL TERRIER

Crest   Skull

Neck   Stop

Withers

Croup   Loin   Back

Muzzle

Shoulder

Hock

Elbow

Stifle or Knee   Forearm

Toes   Pastern

in his eyes lie the expression of the true Jack Russell character: bold, fearless and eager.

EARS: The ears small "V" shaped drop ears carried forward close to the head and of moderate thickness.

The ears should not stand straight up (prick eared). Prick ears are a sign of past infusions of other breeds or are due to thick cartilage. Thick, houndish ears are also not desirable. Ears that have bits missing or are scarred are acceptable when exhibiting the working terrier. The terrier's ears fold over to help him do his job and are meant to protect the inner ear from dirt and other matter in the field.

MOUTH: The mouth should have strong teeth with the top slightly overlapping the lower. (Note: a level bite is acceptable for registration.)

NECK: Clean and muscular, of good length, gradually widening at the shoulders.

FOREQUARTERS: The shoulders should be sloping and well laid back, fine at points and clearly cut at the withers. Forelegs should be strong and straight boned with joints in correct alignment, elbows hanging perpendicular to the body and working free of the sides.

The laid-back angle of the shoulder blade specified in this part of the standard allows good movement of the dog's front end.

BODY: The chest should be shallow, narrow and the front legs set not too widely apart, giving an athletic, rather than heavily chested appearance. As a guide only, the chest should be small enough to be easily spanned behind the shoulders, by average sized hands, when the terrier is in a fit, working condition. The back should be strong, straight and, in comparison to the height of the terrier, give a balanced image. The loin should be slightly arched.

The chest size and shape are of utmost importance. A barrel- or keel-shaped chest would hinder the dog's ability to make its way through narrow passages below ground. A small, flexible chest that can be compressed in a tight place is vital.

HINDQUARTERS: Should be strong and muscular, well put together with good angulation and bend of stifle, giving plenty of drive and propulsion. Looking from behind, the hocks must be straight.

FEET: Round, hard padded, of catlike appearance, neither turning in or out.

Good, compact, well-padded feet are very important to this working dog, as Jack Russells must be able to dig efficiently in a variety of soil conditions.

The tail of the Jack Russell should be set high and carried gaily.

TAIL: Should be set rather high, carried gaily and in proportion to body length, usually about four inches long, providing a good hand-hold.

The approximately 4-inch docked tail provides a good hand-hold for extracting the terrier from an earth tunnel when necessary. Undocked tails carry the risk of breaking while the dog backs up in tiny tunnels, and tails that are too short don't provide a good terrier-handle. A scant one-third of the tail is docked when a puppy is about three days old. Dewclaws are also removed so they don't catch and tear while the dog is working.

COAT: Smooth, without being so sparse as not to provide a certain amount of protection from the elements and undergrowth. Rough or broken coated, without being woolly.

COLOR: White should predominate (i.e., must be more than 51% white) with tan, black, or brown markings. Brindle markings are unacceptable.

White has been the favored color partly because it was thought that hounds would be able to distinguish the terrier from the fox, and partly so that the handler, after digging to the dog, would be able to immediately distinguish the quarry from the dog, even when both are covered in soil.

GAIT: Movement should be free, lively, well coordinated with straight action in front and behind.

PLEASE NOTE: For showing purposes, terriers are classified into two groups 10 inches to 12½ inches, and over 12½ inches and up to 15 inches.

As noted earlier, different heights of dogs were desirable to serve different purposes.

Old scars or injuries, the result of work or accident, should not be allowed to prejudice a terrier's chance in the show ring unless they interfere with its movement or with its utility for work or stud.

Male animals should have two apparently normal testicles fully descended into the scrotum.

A Jack Russell Terrier should not show any strong characteristics of another breed.

Because the Jack Russell is a strain of Fox Terrier, influences from other breeds may surface in markings (such as brindle) or in soft or linty coat textures.

FAULTS: Shyness. Disinterest. Overly aggressive. Defects in bite. Weak jaws. Fleshy ears. Down at shoulder. Barrel ribs. Out at elbow. Narrow hips. Straight stifles. Weak feet. Sluggish or unsound movement. Dishing. Plaiting. Toeing. Silky or woolly coats. Too much color (less than 51% white). Shrill

Responsible people who care about the dog's heritage have bred Jack Russells that are sound, functional and intelligent.

or weak voice. Lack of muscle or skin tone. Lack of stamina or lung reserve. Evidence of foreign blood.

As is evident, the two standards have much in common—both emphasize that the "ideal" dog is one who retains the qualities necessary to be a successful worker in the field. The Jack Russell Terrier has been kept sound, functional, intelligent, and relatively unchanged because of responsible people who have cared about its heritage as a dog capable of work. The standards ask for a correct and balanced terrier.

In connection with the Jack Russell Terrier Club of America, Ailsa Crawford of New Jersey created and set up a registry in the United States that allows only mature dogs over one year to be registered. Even if both parents have passed the standard and are registered, this does not ensure that the offspring will be considered suitable for registration. Each dog is evaluated on its own merit. The dog must have a correct scissor bite, although a level bite is acceptable. Photographs of the dog must be submitted by the club member for registration. The dog must be photographed standing on a hard surface so that its feet can be clearly seen. The front view and both sides of the dog must be shown. This gives the registrar the opportunity to evaluate the appearance of the dog.

The application is secured from the JRTCA. A signed stud certificate and pedigree are required. It is best to include four or more generations.

Perhaps most important, a veterinarian must examine a dog within thirty days of application.

The JRTCA-designed examination certificate covers all aspects of the dogs's basic health as well as genetic conditions that have been specifically noted in Jack Russell Terriers. During the exam it must be established that the dog has normal vision and hearing. Members are encouraged to CERF their dog's eyes and BAER test their dog's ears to assure there are no hidden defects. The dog must be checked for, and declared free of, hearing and eye problems or hernias. The bite is examined. The dog must have a scissor or level bite. A cardiovascular and genitourinary exam is required. It is required that the orthopedic standard of the dog present normal digits that touch the ground. The dog is also checked for luxating patella and evidence of Legg-Perthes, both of which are common to small dogs. The dog must move soundly, free of lameness. The dog must be free of generalized demodectic mange. Evidence of cosmetic surgery must be noted and medical surgery is evaluated. This stringent veterinarian's certification is designed to eliminate from the gene pool of JRTCA-registered dogs any dog that is not suitable for breeding. If the dog does not pass this very complete examination, it may not be registered.

To promote and protect a breed, a wise breeder *never* breeds a dog with any known defect. The JRTCA registry is dedicated to preserving the hearty, healthy strain of working and workable terrier. The dog must be fit in structure and appearance to carry on the tradition of soundness for work.

CHAPTER 4

Finding the Jack Russell Terrier for You

It is important to give serious consideration to the suitability of inviting a JRT into your life. Living with and providing for the needs of this active, alert and bright hunting dog are demanding. If you are not ready to be taken on by a whirlwind of a dog, go no further. You would do well to research another, less demanding dog.

LOCATE A REPUTABLE BREEDER

If you do decide a Jack Russell is for you, seek a reputable breeder that is a member of the Jack Russell Terrier Club of America. Contact the JRTCA by writing to P.O. Box 4527, Lutherville, Maryland 21094-4527. The telephone number is 410-561-3655; the fax line is 410-560-2563. The Jack Russell Terrier Club of America official Web site is www.terrier.com, and you can e-mail the JRTCA at JRTCA@worldnet.att.net. There is a breeder's directory available for sale and the name of the nearest club representative is available by request. The club office has 24-hour-a-day voice mail service.

Find a breeder that breeds from adult JRTCA-registered stock. Be sure the breeder can provide you with a signed pedigree of four or more generations. A signed stud service certificate is the other document that is a must from the breeder. Request information about the JRTCA and be sure the breeder is a member in good standing with the association. Ask the breeder whether he or she agrees with the JRTCA Breeder's Code of Ethics.

Even if you only wish to own a pet and never breed or compete with your dog, get it from a reputable JRTCA breeder. You will do better to have a sound, healthy pet bred from sound, healthy parents. Good breeders are happy when their pups have good homes. Reputable breeders will check you out with as much care as you use investigating them.

Many breeders will not sell to city, condo, or apartment dwellers because of JRTs' unsuitability to these environments. Many will not sell you a dog if you do not have suitable containment or have very young children. Reputable breeders do not engage in breeding for a profit. They care very deeply for the dogs they bring into this world and their concern is to produce the best dogs possible. They breed for attitude, ability and temperament. Their plan includes the desire for excellence in ability to work and appearance.

Good breeders will wait to have several people that want their pups before they even consider breeding. The breeder may intend to keep an offspring. Breeding is an art, and a good breeder

Responsible breeders seek to create dogs that are of good attitude and temperament.

will have a plan and a goal of excellence. You may be asked to pay a deposit to indicate your intention and desire to own one of the planned pups. If you buy a puppy elsewhere, you may lose your deposit.

Responsible breeders will encourage you to join the JRTCA. You may receive information in the puppy package the breeder gives you, or the club will provide it upon request. You will be offered many services as a JRTCA member. The club prints a magazine every other month, along with helpful, informative brochures. Information about the JRTCA should be in a puppy packet with the records of the dog's health care.

Including a dog in your home and life is a huge commitment. You are looking at a relationship that may last many years. You need to consider whether you have the time to devote to a dog. There are also constant expenses associated with maintaining and providing for a pet. Deciding on the breed is only part of the process.

The correct structure of the dog and instincts to work are paramount considerations in any responsible breeding program. The JRT is who it is because it has a history and purpose. It is foremost a hunting dog. It has the courage, bred through generations, to stay below ground to mark the presence of an earthed fox. Everything about this job comes into play with the dog's attitude and appearance.

Taking a puppy into your home requires that you tend to its needs—in many ways this is like having an infant in the house. Pups grow up fast but require your active role as caregiver. They take time to housetrain and to get past the chewing stage. You will have to provide all the necessary immunizations recommended by your veterinarian. Training a puppy is a big effort. It may be very rewarding, but good socialization and training take time and patience. If you are at home a great deal or work from your home, a puppy may be your best choice.

Observe the Breeder's Kennel

If you are purchasing a dog from a breeder, visit the breeder's kennel or home. Ask to see the parents of the puppy if they are on the premises. See as many of the other relatives of the puppy as are available. This offers a good chance to observe the structure and temperament of the dog's relatives.

Beware of overly aggressive dogs. Most JRTs greet intruders with noise—often they are great tiny guard dogs. They are small in size but enormous in spirit. The dogs you visit should settle down and show a happy, confident nature. Overaggression and shyness are not qualities that you want in your puppy.

How are the dogs kept when you visit the breeder? Are the kennels clean, well lit and well ventilated? Do the dogs appear comfortable? Do they seem happy and radiate good health? The best place to see the puppies is right in the breeder's home, where they should be getting lots of human contact. Nothing is sadder than pens or compounds of dogs that receive limited attention. They are deprived of affection and meaningful living. Avoid any animals reared in unfavorable situations.

If the breeder allows visitors to interact with the puppies before eight weeks of age, by all means go play with them. Most breeders are afraid of diseases that may be carried to the pups between the time the immunity from the dam fades and the second puppy shot is given. Do not be surprised if the breeder asks you to leave your shoes outside; many canine diseases are carried to puppies on footwear. Caution is appropriate and may save the lives of the pups.

Look at the puppies. Are they healthy and in clean quarters? Are their eyes clear, and is there no discharge from their noses? Puppies that are raised in the breeder's home get lots of attention and valuable handling. Is the dam with the puppies? She is their greatest teacher. It is healthier for the dam to wean the puppies herself. Pups should be allowed contact with their dam for as long as she chooses. Some dams get weary of pups, while others delight in playing with them.

Work with the Breeder to Find the Right Puppy for You

The character of the dog is very important in the selection process, as you will be living with your choice. A breeder may be helpful and try to match you with the right puppy according to your needs. The experienced, thoughtful breeder is a good guide during the selection process.

The breeder may help you pick out the right puppy for you based on your lifestyle. Your personality and your family's way of living need to be taken into consideration. A boisterous pup may later be a very forward and active adult. Most JRTs are this way, though some pups in the litter may be a bit more laid back, and it's up to you and the breeder to match you with the puppy that will best suit you.

Each puppy has its own personality. Work with the breeder to select a dog whose temperament matches your own. (photo by Jeannie Harrison/Close Encounters of the Furry Kind)

The importance of socialization to the JRT puppy is enormous. Puppies raised in the home or a well-attended kennel are much better prepared to be good pets or working partners. The JRT puppy is a very social animal and thrives with human contact. Buying from a reputable JRTCA breeder may help you avoid the heartaches of health or behavior problems in the dog you purchase.

If You Don't Develop a Rapport, Look Elsewhere

Make sure a contract is written or a good feeling exists between you and the breeder. However, avoid elaborate and complicated breeder contracts that involve control or paybacks of future puppies out of the dog you purchase. You should have a good feeling about the breeder. The good breeder feels you will take good care of his or her "baby" and give the dog a good home.

A responsible breeder will cheerfully help answer any questions about the dog you have purchased at any stage of its life. You may need tips on training or advice on terrier behavior. Your inquiries will never be intrusive to a good breeder. If you feel uncomfortable with the breeder, look further.

When to Buy a Puppy

No pups should be allowed to leave their littermates before eight weeks of age. The first eight weeks are an important, formative period during which the puppy learns social skills and discipline. The JRT is a very social pack dog, and it should never leave its home pack too early.

Jack Russell Terriers are very mouthy at five to eleven weeks or so. They play very roughly and want to chew on everything. Electrical cords are an enormous hazard at this stage. Expect the puppy to try to pull you over by your socks! In hunting,

As tempting as it may be, don't take a puppy home before it is at least eight weeks old. Pups need time with their dam and littermates to learn important social skills. (photo by David Shulman)

this behavior is called "drawing," and is a technique of work in the field. The pattern is already in the terriers' brains at this young age, being hunting dogs from their early beginnings.

Don't be alarmed if you see the dam play very hard in a combative method with the pups. She has distinctive terrier instincts and is teaching strategy to her offspring. The time the dam has with her pups can never be given back if denied. Do not allow it to be disrupted by picking up a puppy early for convenience's sake. Wait until your puppy is fully eight weeks old before taking it away from its home pack to your home.

ACQUIRING AN OLDER DOG

Jack Russell Rescue

If you are away from home for most of the day, it is not a good idea to get a puppy. Puppies need to be fed and let out regularly, and they are far too active and inquisitive to be left alone all day. Instead, consider adopting or purchasing an older dog.

Many people cannot keep a dog because they have to move or experience a change in their living circumstances. It is the function and purpose of Jack Russell Rescue to take these abandoned dogs and rehome them. The rescued dog is a satisfying option. The cost of adoption is low and the rewards are enormous.

The JRTCA Russell Rescue helps displaced and strayed dogs find new homes with approved applicants. No dogs that are known to be aggressive, or that have serious health or behavior

Adopting an adult dog can be enormously rewarding. (photo by Jeannie Harrison/Close Encounters of the Furry Kind)

Through JRTCA Russell Rescue, many lovable dogs are placed in new homes.

problems, are accepted into the program. The dogs that need placement are most often undamaged dogs that are normal, active Jack Russell Terriers. Dogs that show displeasure toward children, if not too extreme, are accepted for placement in adult-only homes. The age of the dog does not matter. All dogs are neutered or spayed prior to adoption. The dogs are given all necessary inoculations and have a current rabies protection certificate.

Each applicant is considered based on what he or she can offer toward the dog's well-being. Many happy matches of dogs to new homes occur on a regular basis.

No rescue dog is adopted out for breeding purposes. The intent is for them to find permanent homes as pets, not to add to the pet overpopulation problem or to contribute more unwanted JRTs. The dog coming into rescue is profiled, and it is determined what situation it will need in a new home. The information is stored in a computer, and the dog's profile is available to rescue volunteers who match dogs with applicants.

Anyone wishing to adopt a dog must first fill out an application to adopt. A call to the Jack Russell Terrier Club of America in Maryland at 410-561-3655 is required to secure an adoption application; voice mail is available twenty-four hours a day. An application may be downloaded from the JRTCA Web site at www.terrier.com. The completed form is mailed to the address on the application. Filling out an application does not guarantee adoption of a dog. The applicant must be able to provide containment and companionship, and a basic understanding of the dog is required. Educational information is included with the application.

Relocation costs are part of the expenses of adopting. If the dog needs to be shipped by air, then air fare must be covered by the adopting family, as must the cost of the airline-approved crate. The releasing family prepares the dog for relocation by taking care of all medical needs and securing a current health certificate. If an adoption is local, a donation is requested to help support JRTCA Russell Rescue.

The family or individual placing the dog in rescue first is instructed to contact the breeder. Breeding dogs is a long-term responsibility, and the breeder may have a suitable home for the dog immediately. Taking the dog back cheerfully helps both the dog and owner. Every breeder should know when one of his or her offspring has come into difficult circumstances. Perhaps the match was inappropriate, or something in the dog's personality needs expert guidance and some retraining to set right.

A terrier may assume a dominant personality and exert undue influence on people that are unaware of how to deal with this trait. If the owner communicates with the breeder, minor phases of undesirable behavior may be adjusted. The dog and the owner can work any problems out and all can be well. Again, this is why buying a dog from a reputable and responsible breeder that honors a breeder's code of ethics is the best possible course of action from the beginning.

Jack Russells seem to have little trouble adapting to a new home—they're confident enough to move right in! (photo by Jean Wentworth)

Most Jack Russell Terriers are flexible and adjust very quickly to their new surroundings and families. The happy-go-lucky attitude of the little Jack Russell helps it in these situations. Most are absolutely sunny about the change of homes. They have a never-look-back attitude. They seem to transmit a feeling of "Hi, I am here, what are we going to do?" They take to their new families almost immediately, if not immediately!

If you already have another dog and you wish to introduce a new dog to your life, there are a few things you should know. Many of the dogs in rescue may get along with the dog you have, but some dogs just are not good living with other dogs. It may be a simple case of just not liking that particular dog, or behavior that designates it an "only dog." It is best to adopt a dog of the opposite gender to promote compatibility. If the dogs

Before getting any breed of dog, it is wise to learn as much as possible about the breed. If you have the energy to keep up with a Jack Russell, this may be the dog for you.

are allowed to meet in a nonthreatening situation, it is more likely they will get along when you bring the new dog home.

ESSENTIALS OF FINDING THE RIGHT DOG

Whether you decide to get a puppy or an older Jack Russell Terrier, remember, the key components to being happy with your new family member are:

Knowing about the breed before you decide it's the one you want.
Getting your puppy from a reputable breeder.
Having the time, energy and facilities to accommodate the feisty Jack Russell Terrier.
Making a commitment to the dog for its lifetime.

CHAPTER 5

Living with a Jack Russell Terrier

Y ou need to look deeply inside yourself and weigh whether you are willing to have your life changed forever by the presence of a Jack Russell Terrier. Life will never be quite the same by having this small in size, huge in spirit white-bodied terrier kick the doors off your quiet life. Jack Russells can look rather humorous and cute, but keep in mind, they are loaded guns.

The JRT will demand that much of your time and energy be spent sharing life with them. Expect a Jack Russell to want to be as physically near you as possible. This is true unless you call it and it does not want to come, or if something more interesting than you has it spellbound. If you doze, your dog will doze. If you as much as think of going outside, expect the dog to jump to its feet.

No doorbell is needed where a JRT lives. Its incredible sense of hearing will alert you when company is arriving or when a neighbor is stirring. Because of their alert nature, Jack Russells are best suited for country life. Any distant bark may be the invitation to a barkathon. Although not yappy, if a JRT has something to express, it will use its voice. Being bred to bay at and mark the presence of quarry below ground, the voice is an important feature of the dog.

Although JRTs are highly adaptable, it is often reported that they become stressed by metropolitan life. Their need for exercise cannot be met with leash walking in a concrete setting. They just do not fare well when kept consistently in apartments or condos. Jack Russell Terriers will adapt to suburban living if a suitable and well-fenced yard is provided. Most behavior problems stem from not meeting the physical and mental needs of this power-packed dog.

To better understand the Jack Russell Terrier, we must constantly consider the dog's function. Everything about the JRT reflects its relationship to working the red fox in dens below ground. Its early inventors had a quick, smart tool in mind with the mastery to do its job. The dog, by design, is energetic and forceful. It serves as a pick ax, shovel, tweezers, and sometimes a hammer and tongs. It takes raw courage to do this work, and this little dog has it. Form follows function with the conformation of the canine worker.

This is a little in-your-face dog. The JRT will not give up hitting the time clock and demanding to have some form of work. If the dog must invent work for itself, you may be in trouble, finding your house torn up while you are gone. If you do not provide a meaningful outlet for the dog's focus, it will invent some activity. JRTs dig, bay, and pursue by genetic programming; expect this bright dog to continue its need to do so if kept as a pet.

THE JACK RUSSELL TERRIER AND OTHER PETS

JRTs and Other Dogs

Jack Russells love their people and, indeed, their people are their pack. They often enjoy the companionship of another JRT of the opposite gender. They form both very strong friendships and very strong aversions. It is a mystery to most of us what happens to spur the aversions. Though they may be best friends with another dog, if one day something goes awry, they are forever enemies.

Jack Russells are very inclined to get in a tussle where the fur flies. Interfemale fighting is classic and often incurable. A détente may last a week or a few months, but fighting will surface again and increase in ugliness.

Characteristic of the JRT is its bullheadedness and overwhelming desire to take out the biggest, strongest dog around. Usually the dog is dark in

If your Jack Russell is an urban dweller, be sure to take it to a dog park where it can really expend some energy. (photo by Michael Schreiber)

color and large enough to cat the JRT on a cracker! This is not isolated to males challenging large males. A little female is just as likely to think she, too, can take down the local Rottweiler or Doberman. The enormous danger is the large dog shaking the little dog and killing it. Never think any Jack Russell will make friends with a big dog without a guided introduction. Part of owning a Jack Russell Terrier involves protecting this brave-to-a-fault dog from its own desire to deal with the world. It is a dog that carves out intent on its own terms.

If you don't keep your Jack Russell busy, you can be sure it will find something to do. (photo by Jeannie Harrison/Close Encounters of the Furry Kind)

JRTs and Cats

Cats seem to be a hobby of the JRT. You can raise a Jack Russell amid cats and think you have a cat-safe dog, but don't believe it. A dog that has been programmed to hunt a fox will turn to hunting cats if a fox is not available. Jack Russells are adaptive dogs. The JRT will show respect to a fox; a cat will not be extended as much courtesy.

JRTs and Birds

Jack Russells are notorious chicken killers. Chickens seem to radiate panic and victim sounds—exactly the type of noise that can frenzy a JRT into a kill. Clearly it is difficult to stop such a pattern of behavior.

Some of our dogs are allowed amid Tony Brown's pet birds. He keeps chickens, peafowl and guinea fowl. One day a young rooster flew into a pen with a bitch and her three pups. When I came upon the scene the mother dog was teaching her whelp to catch. The poor rooster did not have one feather left. The bird was alive, but naked, and unfortunately could not be saved. Believe me when I say it is not suggested to keep birds and JRTs together; it is an exhausting arrangement to manage. This applies to both outdoor and indoor birds.

JRTs and Small Mammals

Pet gerbils or mice are a favorite focus of the JRT. These small mammals may have to live behind

WOODY, THE CAT-FRIENDLY JRT

Woody, a dog I bred from hunting stock, is best friends with the farm cats where he lives. He rolls with them and holds them by their throats and knows when to stop. He is unusual, but he may indeed remain a pal to cats. Woody has his ways, though, and he might behave differently if entered in working trials. His play is rough, and to date, the cats will participate. If, however, a sparrow lands in one of his shrubs, he must stop what he is doing to drive off any bird he sees. His days are filled with patrolling his yard and driving birds away. In a pleasant application, this shows the adaptation of the hunting dog dealing with a nonhunting life. Woody recently took on a groundhog, but has kept his friendship with cats. Not all JRTs have such charming behavior.

closed doors for safety. In such situations, if the dog cannot be found, it is safe to say it will be outside the door where the rodent pet lives. Expect dog dreams to include the break-in of the inner sanctum. A JRT can turn most rodent housing into a fragmented bomb site in seconds. There may not be a cage made to protect any rodent pet from the great white hunter, the JRT.

JRTs and Reptiles and Fish

An iguana is a fascinating creature to Jack Russells. Some will ignore snakes and others will choose to bark at any snake they meet, even through an aquarium. Even fish afford a chance for the JRT to work. Old Nester would sit frozen on the dock until a fish would enter his range. Diving off and attempting to catch the fish was one of his favorite summer vacation activities.

THE JACK RUSSELL TERRIER AND CHILDREN

Introducing a Baby

Most Jack Russells act as if they were the children in the house. Many get their nose out of joint when a child enters the household, and will go to great lengths to

This JRT and cat are playing—but you can never be certain where the play will end and the hunt begin! (photo by Judith Strom)

You can train a Jack Russell to leave chickens and other birds alone, but to succeed, you had best begin this training when the dog is very young.

transition, but with understanding and training, success can be achieved. Often a loving JRT can be found curled up near the baby for warmth and comfort.

Toddlers

As the child grows, we enter another difficult test for a JRT, the toddler stage. This is when most young couples feel they should give up their dog, because conflicts often arise. Small children don't know they are hurting a dog and insulting it when they pull ears or step on paws. The Jack Russell Terrier will usually not tolerate abuse from small children. It does not matter whether the infraction is accidental or intended. Pulling harshly or any rough handling will not be welcomed by most Jack Russells. Some don't mind and just get out of the way when there is an opportunity. Most, however, cannot and will not put up with abuse. This may be linked to their great intelligence. Some choose to hide from small children, while others take on the job of disciplinarian when the adults fail to discipline the unruly child. With children under six years of age, the dog will usually punish in proportion to the perceived offense.

It is not fair to expose this proud dog to abuse from inconsiderate children. Never leave an unruly child and a JRT together unattended. Many dogs are punished by banishment when the child is the guilty offender. Wise breeders do not recommend keeping a JRT in households where the children are under six years of age. That said, there are JRTs that adore little children. Some even allow them to put doll clothes on them, and will hold perfectly

show their displeasure at having the dynamics of their home pack change. This is a time when many owners decide to place their dogs up for adoption, which is sad because many dogs adore and protect "their" babies. It is unfair not to prepare the dog for the baby's arrival, and there are safe and effective ways to do it.

Some people have reported great results from allowing the dog under total supervision to get near the baby and smell and observe it when it arrives home. This seems to satisfy the curiosity of the intelligent dog. The dog must become accustomed to the squeaky sounds of the baby. Some JRTs find the cries of a baby alarming and act nervous. Others are leery of visitors to the baby and assume the role of protector. The dog needs to get used to having your lap shared with someone other than itself. It is not always an easy

Many JRTs adore little children, but be sure to supervise when youngsters interact with your dog.

still until the child releases the dog from the role of doll or baby.

Older Children

Older children tend to fare well with Jack Russells. Some dogs will time the arrival of their children from school and greet them with unbridled adoration. Play time is part of the welcoming. Older, well-mannered children can provide much-needed exercise for the terrier. Intense play can satisfy the needs of physical and mental activity so needed by the dog and the child.

Jack Russells love their family life. Some watch television and love animal shows, which may reflect their intelligence and hunting instinct. David Ross, former chairman of the Jack Russell Terrier Club of America, had a dog that loved the show "Northern Exposure." When the music from the show would begin, the dog would tear from wherever he was, often so fast as to spin out on the highly polished wood floors of the house in order to catch a glimpse of the moose that is part of the opening credits! The dog would join the family to enjoy the show.

TRAINING WITH GAMES AND TOYS

Most Jack Russells love toys as puppies and adults. It is wise to offer a puppy a safe chew toy to satisfy the need to chew as teeth are erupting and as a stress reliever. Dogs love to chew. If you find a dog chewing what it should not be chewing, firmly say "NO" and immediately offer it something appropriate to chew. Be sure to offer praise when the object is accepted in exchange.

Toys can be used to teach the dog to release. Ask the dog to give you the toy, and make a pleasant time of praising for release of the toy to you. Pick one short command and praise the puppy or adult for allowing you to take the toy away. This should be done after the dog has had lots of exercise and is about ready to relax. Teaching a dog to have a soft mouth is a good practice. Never allow biting or nipping of human hands; it gives the wrong message from the start. Jack Russell Terriers

Older children can make great companions for the energetic Jack Russell. Both parties have someone really fun to play with!

people chase the dog and the dog gets under something and guards its prize. It is at first a fun game but can become a battle if not handled well from the start. One of the easiest things to do is distract the dog with some other toy or tidbit, then retrieve the item from its hiding spot. This ensures victory without a battle, and a mode of behavior that is acceptable. Keep things low key and on a pleasant note.

Play at encouraging your JRT to come when called. I cannot stress this enough. Make it a pleasant, rewarding game and learning process, constantly reinforced. From the time they are pups, through life, keep your dogs coming to you. The JRT is a dog that can have a tin ear if its mind is in gear. Keep it in tune by training it to pay attention to you. Get down on the same level as the puppy, even opening your arms as a visual encouragement. Have a bit of biscuit to offer as a reward and lots of praise for a dog that returns to the recall. It may someday save the dog's life—and your nerves!

will play very hard with another dog, but rough play with humans should always be discouraged.

I have found that many people experience a common problem with their Jack Russells: The dog takes things and won't release them. This can be avoided by early training. Many times the treasured item will be a sock or some other prize. The

VISITORS?

When visitors enter the household of a JRT, the dog seems to put out the analyst's couch and evaluate the person rather accurately. Jack Russells either take an immediate liking to the visitor or swagger off. Some will do everything but put a lampshade on their head to be the life of the party; others will cock a leg in disdain of the visitor. Don't buy a used car from anyone your Jack Russell Terrier does not like!

With their playful nature, Jack Russells love toys. A good-sized ball provides hours of amusement. (photo by Judith Strom)

Tug of War

Puppies and adults often enjoy a game of tug of war, but this game can get out of hand if played too roughly. It needs to be fun. By winning on occasion, a puppy gains confidence, which can be good for a dog that tends to be submissive. By training the dog that sometimes you win, you establish yourself as the leader, or in the dog's eyes, the "big dog." You can make tugs out of cotton rope or pick up one of many varieties at any pet supply store. Boda makes some great tugs that terriers find fun. They seem to enjoy the big tugs. It is part of their personality as a big dog in a little dog's body!

Rawhide

Rawhide is offered by some dog owners, but not all. I warn against buying the knotted-ended

rawhide, having had a dog nearly choke to death on an end piece. The large rolled pieces are best to use. They can offer hours of chewing to a happy dog. Always discard the chew when it becomes small enough for a dog to choke on. Look for safe chews that cannot be made into little pieces.

Frisbees and Toy Balls

Many busy dog owners find they can offer some intense exercise with these toys. In a safe play area, these give both owner and dog a chance for some good fun together. This play gives the dog the exercise it *must* have to be a happy, healthy pet.

Be aware that it is not a good idea to leave dogs alone with tennis balls. They have been known to chew them into segments and swallow them. Such an act will require surgery to remove the obstruction. As with young children, never give your dog anything it can rip into pieces small enough to choke the dog or that can create an obstruction to the internal digestive organs. Gumma toys are good, tough toys and take a lot of rough chewing from terriers. Soft rubber toys with squeakers inside are of possible danger, as the squeakers are easily removed by active terrier mouths.

KEEPING A CLEAN HOUSE

Many Jack Russell owners have found training a terrier a true challenge. Without a doubt, these dogs can be very stubborn. You will always know when the dog has a strong opinion, or is, shall we say, pissed off. I have a friend whose file-cabinet bottom rusted as the result of her dog hitting it so many times. Female JRTs can cock a leg as fast and as high as a male. I have had a female that would stand on her front feet to mark higher than any other dog in the pack.

Puppies intuitively want their surroundings to be clean and will generally leave the nest to soil and relieve themselves. Paper training as part of the housetraining routine can ultimately work in your disfavor, as the dog then has to be trained the second time to go outside. Keep any dog on a routine. Feed at the same times daily. Get the dog outside after eating and upon rising. A crate is a good aid to housetraining. Allow the dog to play after a session out and pop it in the crate until it is time to go out again. But use good judgment, and do not overuse the crate or put your dog in the crate as punishment. The crate should serve as a cozy den, with clean washable beddings.

Always praise when the dog does well outside. If an adult dog tends to find an area in the house to soil or mark in, the simple solution is to close the door or use a child gate to prevent problems. (Housetraining is discussed in more detail in Chapter 11.)

RELIABLE CONTAINMENT IS A MUST

Naturally curious and instinctively driven to hunt, a Jack Russell Terrier may decide at any given moment to "do its own thing." Intrigued by

movement and activity, it will follow a noise or a flash of movement in the distance, drawing it to danger and out of the range of the handler's control. This can all happen in seconds, even with the most highly trained Jack Russell. Given the dog's impetuous nature, strong, reliable containment is an absolute must for the Jack Russell owner. JRTs are well known for being bright and resourceful. Some dogs, if left in a well-fenced yard, have mastered climbing the fence, requiring a lid on the containment area! On the other hand, the Jack Russell is a digging dog by its calling, and it can escape through a tunnel dug in a remarkably short time.

Any containment system should be checked on a regular basis to see if canine escape plans are being executed a little at a time, as many unattended dogs decide to leave home in search of adventure. Collars with tags should be removed so they do not catch on the fencing and cause strangulation.

Stockade, wire cyclone and kennel fencing all work well. Burying cement blocks at the base of the fence may help prevent dig-outs. Generally, invisible fencing also works well, but it takes time to teach the dogs where they can and cannot go. Only as a last resort in the training process should you allow the dog to get a signal. Teach the dog by allowing the warning signal, pull the dog back into the safe zone and praise. Use a simple command such as "back." If left untrained, the dog may simply learn to accept the signal in order to set itself free. The flags of the fencing help to train by visual cue. Unfortunately, some dogs may react to the fencing by discontinuing to go outdoors to relieve themselves. Thus, the owner may have to attend outings to help build the dog's confidence until it is comfortable with the limits. Teaching the JRT to be tractable is an ongoing lesson. Patience is always required.

If you choose to install invisible fencing, be sure to frequently check the collar holding the receiver box. Look for frayed areas, as Jack Russells tend to chew on each other's collars. The batteries in the collar must be changed every three months, and it is best to mark the calendar as a reminder. Be aware, moreover, that this system does not keep other dogs away from your dog. If you live in an area where dogs roam freely, extra caution must be taken with invisible fencing. Jack Russell Terriers do not take well to intruders and may even start a fight with a larger dog. Nonetheless, invisible fencing is a very good method of containment while you keep an eye on your dog.

Will this series of barricades keep the puppy enclosed? Time will tell.

Never open a door to let your dog out of containment and think it will be safe for even a minute unattended. There is no guarantee that your vocal command will be enough to get your Jack Russell to come back. Even an obedience-trained JRT will ignore a recall if some other attraction is more enticing. Leash walking is rarely enough exercise for this spring-loaded active dog, and lack of exercise is a primary cause of problem behaviors in Jack Russells.

Expect holes to be dug in any outdoor area in which a JRT is housed. These dogs are terriers, and terriers dig. Rather than getting annoyed by the random holes your JRT will dig in your yard, make both of you happy by setting up an interesting area in which your JRT can spend its time. Jack and Terri Batzer of Maryland have a puppy yard that includes a playground. There is an open barrel and surface tunnels for the young dogs to play in. It is an ideal area for puppies and can be seen from the house. A sandbox provides a great digging outlet, too.

Finally, remember that your dog needs your attention and will not be happy if left alone for prolonged hours. Never leave home with a dog left in a situation from which it could escape or be stolen. Keeping any dog on a trolley line, rope, or chain is inappropriate, and it is especially unsuitable and dangerous for the active Jack Russell. A dog left in this manner is likely to become frustrated and even hostile as a result.

Jack Russell Terriers are dogs that are close to their people. If left alone for hours on end, they feel punished. They are pack dogs and cheerfully

This little dog needs attention and will be unhappy left alone for long periods.

will be contained with a friendly companion of the opposite gender. It is not advised to keep more than two dogs penned together, as they have been known to be hostile amid their own ranks, and there is no anticipating what will set off a fight.

CHAPTER 6

Keeping Your JRT Happy and Healthy

Y ou must provide for the physical needs of your dog by attending to its medical requirements on a regular basis. Keeping your dog happy requires care and attention to its need for lots of human contact and physical activity.

PREVENTIVE CARE

Most health problems are preventable! Vaccinations, a yearly health examination by your dog's veterinarian, good nutrition, adequate daily exercise and loving companionship are the most important things you can provide for your dog to keep it mentally and physically healthy.

As soon as possible after you purchase your puppy or adult dog, you should take it to your veterinarian for a physical examination, any vaccinations that are due, a parasite check and, if necessary, worming. In addition to the pedigree and stud certificate, the breeder or previous owner should have provided you with the dog's health records, current through the date of purchase.

Puppies need to be wormed and should have their first immunization before leaving the breeder's facility. Find out what the breeder has provided and bring a copy of the records to your veterinarian when you take the new pup for its first visit.

Make your trip to the veterinarian a pleasant one. You should not act nervous or make a fuss over the trip or any procedure, as your terrier will be sure to pick up on your feelings. Your dog's introduction to its doctor should be very matter-of-fact. That said, let's take a look at the parasites, diseases and genetic problems that most commonly afflict Jack Russell Terriers.

INTERNAL PARASITES

Controlling worms is a concern throughout the dog's life. The breeder will begin worming the pups at two to three weeks of age. Whatever worms the pups have will be passed in their feces. The treatment should be repeated at least once

Your breeder will begin the process of worming his or her puppies. After that, it's up to you to see to it your puppy is treated for worms. (photo by Jeannie Harrison/Close Encounters of the Furry Kind)

again within the next two weeks. A third, or even fourth, treatment will be necessary if worms are found after the previous treatments.

Roundworms

Roundworms will be present in a puppy if the dam has ever had them (which is likely regardless of the level of care she may have received). Some roundworm larvae encyst in tissue and, in the late stages of pregnancy, the dormant larvae are released and carried to the unborn pups, passing through the breast milk of the dam. It is advisable to deworm a bitch before she is bred, and most breeders do; however, even by worming her, the encysted larvae will not be eliminated. Adult female roundworms can lay up to 200,000 eggs a day, which are passed in a dog's feces. Early treatment, regular fecal checks and good sanitation are vital to stem a round-worm infestation.

Hookworms

It is uncommon for a puppy to born with hookworms, but these parasites can be acquired through the mother's milk during the first two or three weeks of life. Left untreated, an affected puppy can die. Hookworms live in the small intestine, where they "hook" onto the intestinal wall and suck blood. Bloody diarrhea is usually the first sign of a problem. Hookworm eggs are passed through feces. The same medication used for roundworms is used to treat hookworms.

Whipworms

Adult whipworms live in the large intestine, where they feed on blood. The eggs are passed in the stool and can live in the soil for many years. If your dog eats the fresh spring grass, or buries its bone in the yard, it can pick up eggs from the infected soil. Heavy infestations cause diarrhea, often watery or bloody. The dog may appear thin. Unfortunately, whipworms can be difficult to detect, as they do not continually shed eggs.

Tapeworms

Probably the most familiar internal parasite for dog owners to encounter is the tapeworm. There are different kinds of tapeworms, but the most common is transmitted by fleas. Fleas typically harbor tapeworm eggs, which get passed to the dog when it bites or swallows the flea. Tapeworms can also be acquired by eating raw animal parts, such as mice or other dead animals your JRT may encounter or kill in its travels. The eggs hatch and worms grow inside the dog's body. Unlike some other worms, owners can usually detect a tapeworm infestation in their dog because they will notice the worms in their dog's feces. Tapeworm segments look like small, white grains of rice in or on a dog's feces. By the time you see segments in the feces or in the hair around the dog's anus, there is a probably a fairly heavy infestation. Consult your veterinarian immediately.

Heartworm

Heartworm is a very serious affliction that, fortunately, can be easily prevented. Heartworm larvae enter your dog's bloodstream from a bite from an infected mosquito. The larvae mature into adult worms in your dog's heart. Heartworms can grow to be quite long, and an infestation can quickly clog the heart.

Dozens of heartworms, up to twelve inches long, have been found in the heart of just one dog. There may be no symptoms of infestation for several years. Even at an advanced stage, the early symptoms may be misinterpreted, and often by this time the infestation can prove fatal. Treating an infestation of heartworms involves poisoning the worms, which can be as hard on your dog as on the parasites. This is why prevention is vital for the health and safety of your dog. Blood must be drawn and tested to assure that your dog is free from infection. If the dog is not infected, the veterinarian will prescribe a heartworm preventive to be given in monthly doses, or he may devise another schedule. In warm climates the preventive must be given all year. In colder climates where mosquitoes are inactive for several months, you may be able to discontinue treatment during the colder months. Your veterinarian will advise you as to the procedure suggested in your area.

EXTERNAL PARASITES

Fleas

Fleas are a most annoying problem to dogs. Flea "dirt" found in the dog's coat may sometimes be spotted more easily than the fleas themselves. The flea "dirt" is digested dog blood and can be seen as dark specks in the dog's coat. If moistened, it becomes a rusty reddish color, distinguishing it

Prevention is the key to keeping your dog healthy. (photo by Winter Churchill Photography)

from soil. The saliva of the flea is very irritating to dogs allergic to it, and will cause them to break out in a rash and suffer what is known as flea allergy dermatitis. Itching becomes so severe that hair loss is sometimes noted at the base of the tail and on the inner thighs and back of the hind legs from scratching and biting.

Fleas prefer a warm, humid environment. Having fallen off the dog and found a suitable place to incubate, it takes only a few days for their eggs to hatch into larvae. The larvae spin a cocoon, go into a pupal stage and emerge in two to three weeks. This stage can also take up to several months. After hatching, the fleas go in search of food. If they cannot find any, they can go without it for many months. This is an important reason to rid your home and kennel of these parasites. Do not allow fleas to live on your dog. As soon as your terrier walks by and provides a meal for the flea, the life cycle of the flea begins all over again. One female flea can lay thousands of eggs in her lifetime.

The life cycle of the fleas must be broken to be rid of them. To eradicate fleas, the home and yard must be treated as well. Most veterinarians can supply you with "flea bombs" for the home. Be prepared to thoroughly vacuum the floors and furniture in your home. Dispose of the vacuum cleaner bag immediately. If your dog has a serious infestation, bathe it with a flea shampoo. Comb dogs with a fine-toothed flea comb daily during flea season. Keep a dish of soapy water on hand so you can put the fleas in it, thus coating and killing them. Remember, fleas are remarkable athletes and can jump enormous distances for their tiny size.

Because fleas are such a common and annoying problem, there are many treatments available to control them. Some are administered orally, others topically. Because of the wide range of products available, and their varying ingredients, it's best to discuss which product is most effective for your dog with your veterinarian.

Ticks

Ticks are pesky external parasites that present a continuous and potentially serious, even deadly, problem for your terrier. Ticks of various species may attach themselves to your dog. The brown dog tick is the most common and can cause such ailments as Rocky Mountain spotted fever and

An active field dog like the Jack Russell is bound to be exposed to ticks. Make a point of looking your dog over very carefully every time you come in from the great outdoors.

canine ehrlichiosis. Deer ticks and other ticks carry the debilitating Lyme disease. Most often, ticks will be found on the dog's ears, neck or head, or even between the toes. If you spot ticks on your terrier, remove them. Dip a cotton ball or swab into rubbing alcohol or nail polish remover, and dab that on the tick to numb it. Wait a few minutes for it to loosen its grip; then, with tweezers, grasp the tick as close as possible to the dog's skin and firmly pull it out. Make sure the head and mouth parts are removed. Clean the area with antiseptic and dress with an antibiotic ointment.

Lyme disease is a bacterial infection spread by ticks, which are most prevalent in late spring and summer. The disease affects both dogs and humans. The tick must be attached to a dog or person for at least twenty-four to forty-eight hours before there is a significant risk of infection. The disease has three stages. A painless, red rash occurs at the site of the bite about a week and a half after exposure. This stage may be accompanied by a low-grade fever and flu-like symptoms. The second stage of illness follows days to weeks later with more rashes, neurological and heart disorders or musculoskeletal pain. A year later the infection involves the nervous system and joints. Symptoms are chronic and progressive. Antibiotic treatment can be effective.

Avoid exposure to ticks by wearing protective, preferably light-colored clothing. Apply tick repellent to yourself and your dog. When you leave an area where there are ticks, check immediately to see if there are any on you or your dog. Check again a few hours later. If you develop a suspicious rash, see your doctor immediately.

VACCINATIONS

There are a number of diseases that can be prevented by vaccinating your puppy or dog. The first vaccinations should be given to your puppy at about eight weeks of age, when the immunity provided by the dam declines. The second set of vaccines should be given at twelve weeks, and the third at sixteen weeks. These inoculations will protect your dog from distemper, hepatitis, leptospirosis, parvovirus, coronavirus and parainfluenza (kennel cough). Protection given annually is necessary for the continued good health of your dog.

Distemper

Distemper kills puppies and dogs that have not been immunized against it. The disease spreads easily from one dog to another and results in loss of appetite, diarrhea, discharge from the nose and eyes and a dry cough. A dog that does survive distemper can suffer from permanent damage to both the brain and nervous system.

Canine Hepatitis

Canine hepatitis spreads by contact with infected dogs. The urine, feces or saliva of the infected dog can spread the disease. It affects the liver, kidneys and lining of the blood vessels. There may be a discharge from the eyes, mouth and nose, and it is often difficult to distinguish hepatitis from distemper.

Leptospirosis

Leptospirosis is often transmitted to dogs from the urine of infected rats. Because Jack Russells often spend much of their time in barns and stables, exposure to leptospirosis is likely. Rats frequent barns where grains are stored. Be certain your dog is protected from this disease, which damages the liver, kidneys and digestive tract. The symptoms include pain, depression, sores in the mouth, vomiting, diarrhea and a yellow color in the eyes.

Parvovirus

Parvovirus is a contagious viral disease transmitted by infected fecal matter carried on dogs. It may be carried on paws, hair, cages, and even an owner's footwear. Parvovirus is a killer of puppies. The illness may begin with a loss of appetite, depression and vomiting. The disease progresses to diarrhea, often bloody, and fever. Parvo may strike in forms that damage the heart or attack the gastrointestinal tract. It can even bring on congestive heart failure.

Keeping your dog's vaccinations current will go far to maintain its health. Don't neglect this extremely important aspect of caring for your JRT.

Where there has been an outbreak of parvo, the dog's living space should be cleaned and disinfected with diluted chlorine bleach solution.

Kennel Cough

Kennel cough does not kill, but it can make a dog more susceptible to other infections. It is highly contagious, and any affected dog should be isolated to contain the illness. Your veterinarian will suggest antibiotics and keeping the dog in a warm, humid environment until it recovers. There are several viruses that cause kennel cough. Both the parainfluenza and bordetella vaccines help to prevent spreading this affliction. Kennel cough may be contracted where a number of dogs are housed or congregate in a confined environment. When you take your dog to terrier trials, be sure to have it vaccinated beforehand.

Rabies

When your puppy reaches four to six months of age, it will need its first rabies shot. After that, depending on the type of shot given, the vaccine will need to be readministered either every year or every third year. If your dog is exposed to wildlife or you are in an area with an outbreak of deadly infectious rabies, more frequent protection may be recommended or required.

Rabies is a fatal disease affecting the nervous system. It can be transmitted through infected saliva to humans and other animals from a bite or through a cut or scratch on the skin. Nearly all warm-blooded animals can carry the virus. It is common in foxes, skunks, raccoons and bats. Jack

Russells are bred to locate these kinds of animals, and often encounter wildlife at unexpected times. Never allow your dog to be unprotected from rabies—by keeping your dog immunized, you also protect yourself. There is no effective treatment for dogs exposed if unprotected.

Symptoms of rabies exposure may manifest as a change in temperament. Eyes may become sensitive to light, and the dog may seek seclusion. Upon withdrawing, the dog may show signs of aggression. Lack of coordination and loss of facial muscle control are other advanced symptoms. Coma and death will follow. Rabies is easy to prevent by inoculation, and it is critical that your dog's vaccinations be kept current.

Mange is contagious from one animal to the next, and a working JRT is a good candidate. An infected dog should be taken to the veterinarian immediately.

Sarcoptic Mange

No mention of the working terrier can be complete without mentioning mange. Even puppies playing in holes in fields may pick up the disorder. It is highly contagious and can be contracted by the dog entering earth where a fox or other animal with mange has dwelled. It is caused by a microscopic insect called a mite. Mange appears in many areas of the country and is frequently contracted by red foxes. It may appear first on the face, ears, belly or thighs of the dog, and spread with itchy patches of missing hair. The skin will be scabby looking. The mite feeds and reproduces on the dog. People can catch mange, too, but fortunately, the mite cannot complete its life cycle on humans. It can cause a great deal of itching until cured, however. It is paramount to cure the dog of mange for both the comfort of the dog and the protection of the owner. If you suspect your dog is infected, see your veterinarian immediately.

DEFECTS AND DISORDERS

All creatures carry some defective genes, and approximately 500 genetic disorders have been identified in dogs. Many breeds are cursed with a large number of dogs that suffer from problems such as dysplasia and luxated patellas (knees). Fortunately, the number of problems and affected dogs have been well controlled in the Jack Russell Terrier population. The good health of the JRT is related to the broad-based genetic makeup of the dog. Also, the JRTCA policy of limiting inbreeding has truly helped the breed.

Explains George Padgett, DVM, a canine genetic specialist, veterinary pathologist and author of *The Control of Canine Genetic Diseases* (Howell Book House, 1998):

> *The risk for genetic disease in dogs is much higher than the risk of genetic disease in people because of the way we've bred dogs. The risk for mating between second cousins is ⅓ of 1 percent, but the risk of producing a defect from any given trait if you mate father-daughter, mother-son, or brother-sister is 12½ percent—33 fold more risky. In dogs, we commonly breed closer than second cousins, and the closer the relationship, the greater risk.*

The practice of inbreeding does make for an increase in problems. The strict inbreeding policy of the Jack Russell Terrier Club of America's breed registry is to protect the dog from what has occurred in many other breeds from close breeding.

Bite Defects

Some of the defects that have been seen in Jack Russell Terriers are related to the dog's bite. An undershot bite was listed as the most common defect in the breeder's survey that was recently sent to JRTCA breeders. Overshot mouths have also been reported.

Deafness

Deafness, both unilateral (one ear) and bilateral (both ears), follows bite defects in prevalence.

Before two Jack Russell Terriers are mated, both should have a BAER test performed. According to Dr. George M. Strain:

> *The hearing test, known as the Brainstem Auditory Evoked Response (BAER) or Brainstem Auditory Evoked Potential (BAEP), detects electrical activity in the cochlea and auditory pathways in the brain in much the same way an antenna detects radio or TV signals or an EKG detects electrical activity of the heart. The response waveform consists of a series of peaks numbered with Roman numerals: Peak I is produced by the cochlea and later peaks are produced within the brain. The response from an ear that is deaf is an essentially flat line.*
>
> *Tiny electrodes are placed under the skin of the dog's scalp: one in front of each ear, one at the top of the head, and one between and behind the eyes. It is rare for a dog to exhibit any pain from the placement of the electrodes. If anything, the dog objects to the gentle restraint and the irritation of wires hanging in front of its face. The stimulus click produced by the computer is directed into the ear with a foam insert earphone. Each ear is tested individually, and the test usually is complete in 10–15 minutes. Sedation or anesthesia are usually not necessary unless the dog becomes extremely agitated, which can usually be avoided with patient and gentle handling. A printout of the test results, showing the actual recorded waveform, is provided at the end of the procedure. Test results are confidential.*

By BAER testing their dogs, responsible breeders can protect the future of the breed by helping keep serious defects such as deafness out of the gene pool.

Missing Testicle

A monorchid dog has one testicle in the scrotum. Although such a dog is fertile, it should not be bred because this is a known inherited defect. A cryptorchid dog has no testicles in the scrotum, and is sterile.

Primary Lens Luxation

Primary lens luxation, a condition in which the lens of the eye becomes displaced, has been seen in Jack Russell Terriers. It is both painful and causes blindness. Dislocation of the lens may occur from hereditary predisposition or from an injury. The dislocation may be partial (subluxated) or complete (luxated).

Dogs used for breeding should be CERF (Canine Eye Registration Foundation) tested each year. By testing and not breeding dogs with any

Responsible breeders have their dogs tested for genetic defects and will breed only healthy, sound animals.

known eye problems, breeders help work toward a goal of eliminating heritable eye diseases in dogs. Your veterinarian can advise you where your dog can be CERF tested, or you can call Purdue University at (317) 494-8179.

Patellar Luxation

Patellar luxation is a problem in some Jack Russell Terriers. The patella is a small bone within the tendon of the quadriceps femoris muscle. It can be compared to the kneecap in humans, so you can think of patellar luxation as similar to a "trick knee." A dog with this condition may appear from the rear to having a hopping gait, but this sign does not always manifest itself. Obviously, a JRT suffering from this condition will not excel at working or hunting. All affected animals should be eliminated from breeding. Your veterinarian is able to test for luxing patellas. This is required prior to registration with the JRTCA as part of the screening process during application on the vet certificate.

Other Genetic Problems

Umbilical and inguinal hernias have been reported by breeders, and missing premolars have also been noted in Jack Russell Terriers.

On occasion, Von Willebrand's disease is found in JRTs. If you see signs of excessive bleeding in teething pups or abnormal bleeding in puppies or adult dogs, call your veterinarian right away.

Finally, aggressiveness is another defect that has been seen in the breed.

Breeders that are willing to share their knowledge can protect a breed through better understanding and education. One way to protect a breed is never to breed any dog with any known defect. The disorders listed above are all serious defects, and even the most conscientious breeders will see defects from time to time. Some may surface that have not been seen previously in a line—often due to the combination of a particular male and female. The breeding should never be repeated. If its disorder is not debilitating, the dog or bitch can be neutered or spayed and kept as a pet. (For more on genetics and breeding, see Chapter 12.)

SPAYING AND NEUTERING

Neutering or spaying is the kindest thing you can do for your dog. And life with a dog is much easier for you, too, if you do not have to be concerned with the problems associated with the female's heat cycles or the male's compulsion to seek a female in season.

If a female is spayed at about six months of age, she is at virtually no risk of developing breast cancer. Because spaying involves removal of the uterus and ovaries, the danger of cancer in those organs is removed with them. Spaying also eliminates the mess associated with bleeding and the problems involved with having to isolate her for three to four weeks, twice a year, to keep her away from unneutered males. A bitch in season cannot be allowed out of your sight for even a moment.

Keeping her in a kennel run or wire crate is no guarantee that a male will not get to her.

The female in heat has a strong desire to get to a male and her scent will attract unwanted males from far and wide. But this is just hormones and instinct at work. She has no innate "desire" to have babies. It is more than a misconception, it is simply untrue, that by allowing a bitch to have a litter she will be more "fulfilled" or become a better pet. A spayed bitch is more even in temperament than one who is cycling. And fights between female JRs often come up around the onset of heat cycles—a situation made worse by the fact that females living in the same household tend to cycle at about the same time.

Having an intact male in the house comes with its own set of problems, not the least of which is his tendency to mark his territory, inside the house as well as out. If he can detect a female in heat (his great sense of smell will let him know who is in season within a very large area) he will not only become a more prolific marker, he will become very restless and vocal in his cries. He may even lose his appetite. An intact male will go to great lengths to escape confinement, possibly harming himself in his efforts to locate the female.

Spayed and neutered animals will not become fat and lazy unless you let them. About the time when spaying and neutering can be done, the dog is nearing maturity and needing an adjustment in the type and amount of food being served. By keeping the diet appropriate to age and activity level, your dog will not get fat.

CHAPTER 7

Caring for the Jack Russell Terrier

An important component of preventive care is making sure all the working parts of your working terrier are in good order. Keeping ears, eyes and teeth clean and healthy is important. Also vital to your dog are proper nutrition and exercise. All these elements of care will be covered in this chapter.

FEEDING YOUR JACK RUSSELL TERRIER

Good nutrition is essential to the good health of your dog. People may have different opinions on feeding, but all will agree on the need for proper nutrition. The nutritional needs of the dog change during its life depending on what growth stage it's in and whether it is particularly active or is being bred.

When deciding on what to feed your JRT, speak to your dog's breeder, to other JRT owners and to your veterinarian. Premium food should always be chosen; less expensive foods may contain fillers, artificial colors and additives. Store and discount brands should probably be avoided, but relatively low-cost, high-quality foods are available both in grocery and feed stores. Read and compare labels. By seeking quality and palatability in dog food, you will be able to provide the best food available for your terrier.

Feeding Puppies

Puppies start life on the dam's milk, and are weaned at between five and six weeks of age. Timing will depend on the dam's willingness to nurse and the practices of the breeder. As the deciduous or milk teeth begin to erupt, the pups may be discouraged by the dam when she's nipped by these sharp little teeth. While the pups are still nursing, at around four weeks, the breeder will begin to feed them fine-textured, well-moistened gruel to acclimate them to solid food.

In many of these first feedings, the pups cover themselves with the gruel and walk in it. It can make quite a mess. At about this stage, given the clean-ups after feeding and the resulting soiling, one finds the pups quite a responsibility, requiring frequent swabbing of the decks!

Before long the pups catch on and are eating heartily, with less trashing of the puppy area. As they progress in their eating, so, too, does the breeder progress in feeding them more solid food. By the time pups are ready to join their new families, at around eight to ten weeks of age, they are fully weaned off their dam and on to puppy food. Your pup's breeder will tell you what he or she has been feeding so that you can disrupt your puppy's food and schedule as little as possible. If you want to change foods, do so gradually.

Feeding the Adult Dog

Feeding a dog in its prime is easy. There are many well-formulated dog foods on the market. Avoid food with added color and unnecessary ingredients. Some JRTs don't do well on food high in

Start your puppy on whatever it was being fed by its breeder—you can change over to another food gradually.

soy. Any dog with a tendency toward allergies will react better to a premium food without added ingredients such as coloring and preservatives. For younger dogs, the food should contain approximately 23 to 26 percent protein. A mature dog will thrive on about 20 percent protein. Don't allow the dog to become too thin or too fat. If the dog is working or active with agility or any performance activity, feed accordingly.

Fat content in dog food is another consideration. Dogs that are worked or housed in outdoor kennels in cold weather may thrive on a higher fat content, perhaps 15 percent. Dogs, and even puppies, that are housed indoors, as well as older dogs, will do very well on food with a fat content of around 10 percent.

Never feed your Jack Russell from the table. First, table scraps should be less than 25 percent of the dog's dietary intake. Sure, your dog will love eating what you eat, and food is as delightful to

There are a number of good-quality dog foods on the market that will keep your JRT fit.

food. By monitoring your dog's meals, you can find out if your dog is not feeling well. If your dog normally breezes through meals but either picks or doesn't eat one day, you should suspect something is wrong and be prepared to take it to the veterinarian.

If you feed biscuits or treats, be mindful of the total of these added treats to the dog's daily caloric intake. An inactive dog can gain weight quickly from treats. A quick way to determine if your terrier is carrying too much weight is to put your hand over its back, thumb on one side, fingers on the other, and run your hand lightly down the back. You should be able to feel the individual ribs, but you should not be able to see them.

the dog as it is to you, but it will stay healthiest on a diet of premium dog food. Second, you don't want to get your dog into any bad habits, and begging at the table is one of them. Even if you and your family don't mind, your dog's persistence may annoy company. Get your dog used to lying down on its bed while you eat. If you want to give it a tasty leftover, put the food in the dog's bowl and call it over after you have finished your meal.

Free-choice feeding (allowing the dog to snack or pick at its leisure by leaving its bowl of food down all day), is another poor practice. It is best to feed a dog and pick up any uneaten food in ten minutes. If feeding more than one terrier, crate them for meal time. By crating, you can monitor the intake of each dog and avoid any conflict a dominant dog may exert over another to take its

It is more common to see an overweight dog than an underweight one. However, some owners have the idea that a thin dog looks fit. This is incorrect. The dog must be in good condition, well muscled and nourished for optimum health. The appearance of your dog is the best indicator of good nutrition.

Supplements

Don't give supplements unless they are prescribed by your veterinarian for some indicated reason. All good-quality dog foods labeled as "complete" will provide all that your dog needs nutritionally. There may be special circumstances, such as pregnancy and lactation, in which your dog may require some addition of one or more nutrients, but add them only on the recommendation of your veterinarian.

Your dog's appearance—which should be well muscled, neither too thin nor too heavy—is a good indication of whether its nutritional needs are being met.

Casual supplementation can cause imbalances and unexpected problems. It is not a good practice to think more of a good thing is necessarily better.

The food you give your Jack Russell Terrier should contain protein, fat, carbohydrates, fiber, vitamins and minerals, all in proper quantities and in proportion to each other. Quality food will have the nutrients your dog needs for healthy growth, development and maintenance.

Feeding Your Older JRT

Older dogs sometimes become less active. Often it is difficult to tell an older JRT from a young one, except for a bit of graying on the face color. As a rule, Jack Russells stay active into their senior years. To keep an older dog healthy, watch its weight carefully, adjusting the intake of food accordingly. Take care not to allow the older dog to get fat and out of condition. The dog should have a good covering of flesh but not be fat.

EAR CARE

The breed Standard for the Jack Russell Terrier calls for an ear that is small, "V"-shaped, carried forward close to the head and of moderate thickness. In theory, the fold over the ear helps keep dirt out of the inner ear when the dogs toils in soil below ground.

If you see your terrier puppy or adult repeatedly shaking its head or scratching at its ears, this is a sign something may be wrong with the health of the ears. An unpleasant odor can indicate infection or ear mites. If ear mites are present, your veterinarian will prescribe ear drops. It is important for the health of your dog to eliminate ear mites. They are highly contagious, and all pets in the home will need to be checked and possibly treated if one dog has mites.

Check to see the dog's ears are not clogged with soil. Terriers have a tendency to get soil in their ears. You may choose to use a liquid ear-cleansing product. Clean your terrier's ears with a cotton swab, taking care *never* to insert the swab farther into the ear than you can see.

EYE CARE

Eye care is important to the Jack Russell Terrier that works below ground and is prone to having soil work into the eyes while digging. Even a dog poking at a hole may end up with dirt and sand in its eyes that, if not removed, can scratch the

The way a JRT's ear folds over helps to protect the inner ear from dirt. (photo by Winter Churchill Photography)

TOOTH AND MOUTH CARE

Clean, healthy teeth contribute to the overall good health of your dog. Brushing teeth in puppies gets them used to it without protest rather quickly. If you keep the sessions short and pleasant, the dog will find the attention favorable. Use only pastes formulated for dogs. Unlike humans, dogs cannot spit out the paste deposited by the brushing. Toothpaste designed for humans is *not* formulated for dogs.

Tartar deposits build up quickly, particularly on the canine teeth and the upper molars. Neglect can lead to gum disease and the loss of teeth. Working terriers often have missing, pulled or broken teeth as the result of pulling roots in tunnels. Brushing is the perfect opportunity to check your dog's mouth on a regular basis.

Tooth scalers are available from canine products catalogs. You can purchase dog toothbrushes shaped for the canine mouth and toothpaste designed for dogs, or you may wrap gauze around your finger and brush with it.

Have your dog's teeth checked at least once a year by the veterinarian. It may be necessary to have them thoroughly cleaned by the vet. The dog may be put under sedation for the procedure to make it easier and faster for the doctor to clean and polish the teeth. Discuss the procedure with your veterinarian.

A blood test is advised for dogs over five years old to determine whether the dog's internal organs are up to the rigors of anesthesia. Older dogs tend to have buildup on their teeth that can cause bad breath.

corneas. You can wash out the eyes with lukewarm water, a solution of boric acid or a special eye-cleaning preparation. Pull the lids back to make sure no dirt is hiding in the corners of the eyes or under the lids.

When you need to apply eye drops or a topical ophthalmic ointment to your dog's eyes, hold its head against your chest, tip the head upward and pull down the lower eyelid to apply the medication. The Jack Russell is small enough that one person can handle the procedure easily. Check with your veterinarian regarding the solution suggested for caring for your working terrier's eyes. Use only the ointment the veterinarian prescribes.

Your terrier's teeth should be examined annually by your veterinarian.

Bad breath on a dog of any age may indicate a dental problem. Neglected teeth may lead to periodontal disease. The bacteria can enter the bloodstream and are associated with other diseases of the heart, liver and kidneys. Red or bleeding gums are an indication of a problem that requires a prompt visit to the veterinarian.

Maintaining good dental hygiene may help the senior dog chew its food. Check the mouth of the older dog and if tartar has built up or gums are puffy, get the teeth cleaned by your veterinarian. Sometimes watering kibble to soften it a bit helps

the older dog, which may have worn or missing teeth from a career of work. Hard kibble, however, does help keep teeth cleaner and gums healthy.

EXERCISING YOUR JACK RUSSELL TERRIER

Some claim it is nearly impossible to tire a Jack Russell. They have boundless energy and must have an outlet for it. Leash walking a couple of times a day just is not going to do. This is a dog that needs major movement daily to stay mentally healthy. The JRT is a work in motion. These dogs dig holes and can make a back yard look like a bomb site. If fenced, they will run the line of the fence so no grass will grow along their expressway. They bounce and jump as if on spring-loaded legs. If their exercise needs are not met, they have a tendency to create what we interpret as trouble.

One of the most common problems with JRTs is they will exercise themselves if you don't. They may take off on an unauthorized run in the split second you turn your back. If they return, they will seek their crate and rest. Quickly refreshed, the dog will again be ready to go in a heartbeat. The humans involved in such escapades will be both exhausted and cranky.

A JRT will also hunt for exercise when it gets away from its owners. If it gets a distance away off-leash, it will go until its needs are met. If it encounters a den with scent and a resident, the owner's search for the dog will be complicated by the dog not being visible above ground. If this happens to you, one of the best things to do is simply walk and listen. Often the dog will give an

These two Jack Russells are ready to spring into action.

intermittent bark or bay that can be heard. In cases when the dog is deep, another dog with its keen hearing may take you to where the first dog is located if luck is with you.

The Jack Russell Terrier is a willful dog that can truly be a handful to keep in control. There may be no way to avoid trouble with a JRT that dreams of escape. Perhaps the dog's needs are not being met in limited containment. Jack Russells love to run free. It is very dangerous for a dog to get away from the control of the handler. These dogs are not wise to traffic. They never look to see impending disaster in the form of a car or truck. Prevention by exercising your dog in a safe enclosure is helpful, but may still not be enough for your JRT.

Some people never let their terriers run free, from accumulated bad experiences. It is difficult for this dog that needs an enormous amount of exercise to have no opportunity to run free. This is

another reminder for those dwelling in apartments or condos, or those without a safe yard, not to get a Jack Russell Terrier. You will not be able to meet the needs of this dog's demand for exercise.

A game of ball or Frisbee for at least half an hour twice a day may provide almost enough exercise. If you jog or bicycle, and take the dog on a tether, you both will be in good shape. Expect a long ride or a very long jog to satisfy the needs of the terrier. A safe place for a terrier to uncork by running is ideal. A country setting away from traffic is the best place for the dog to run and explore with its nose and eyes. The dog's mind thrives with

A country setting that a terrier can safely explore will delight your dog. (photo by Winter Churchill Photography)

exercise and stimulation, but its safety should always be the prime concern.

A dog that has been taught to return to its handler is much more fun to let run free. Nothing is more upsetting than a dog that runs off, unresponsive to the handler's call. Make certain the dog will return to you. The call of the scents and sounds in the field is a great temptation to the active, intelligent mind of the Jack Russell. Sometimes, when a dog turns a deaf ear, one can feign great excitement in a tone of voice that draws the dog quickly to see what the handler is so excited over. Take warning, though: the smart JRT quickly learns when you are acting and using a ploy.

The best possible exercise for the Jack Russell Terrier is hunting. It is what these dogs love the most and what they have been bred to do. It is the one form of exercise that cools their jets for up to two days! Digging is what they love to do and what they are built for. Expect holes in your yard—which are a small price to pay for a happy terrier. You can allow one hole and discourage others from being dug. Most of the time JRTs love to dig where you have just dug. If you plant something in their area, expect to find it dug up faster than you planted it.

TAKING YOUR JRT WITH YOU

Most Jack Russell Terriers really enjoy rides in the car or on anything that moves. Take them along with you when there is no danger from extreme temperatures in the car. They like watching from windows and may feel they have to protect their car in your absence. Giving them the chance to be part of your routine is very satisfying to them. Their preference is to go anywhere you go. They are dogs that want your company and to be near you. They prefer anything interesting you may do that is filled with action. If you rest, they may follow suit and rest when you do. You may find you have a shadow much of the time. If something more interesting than you unfolds, however, expect them to be in on the action, with or without you.

BEWARE OF OVERHEATING YOUR JRT

Remember that no dog should be left in a car, even with the windows partially open. The dangers of overheating are great, especially in the summer months. If your dog suffers from heat stroke, either from too much activity or from being left in a hot place, take action immediately. Cool down the dog as quickly as possible by hosing it for at least fifteen minutes before rushing it to the veterinarian. You may run cool water over the dog in the sink or bathtub. If you don't respond quickly, your dog may expire before you get it to the veterinarian. By *never* leaving your dog in a hot car, and by keeping an eye on it when outside in the summer, you can greatly reduce the likelihood of its suffering from heatstroke.

Going along for the ride brings your JRT great satisfaction. (photo by Jean Wentworth)

REST—IS IT POSSIBLE FOR A JRT?

Jack Russells will recuperate very quickly from a hard day's work. Often when they have put in a hard hunt and carry the marks of battle, they will sleep a few days and be stiff and sore but bounce back ready to do it all again. Fast to recover from exertion, some dogs will get recharged by a cat nap. Many marvel at the endless energy the JRT possesses.

A friendly crate will be a welcome lair for the dog to rest in. The crate door may be left open, with comfortable clean bedding inside. The dog will seek this place to rest. Many note that a Jack Russell Terrier will just as happily take to your bed. Often, if allowed to do so, it will beat you to bed and be found on your pillow. Some JRTs are "outties" and some are "innies": Outties sleep on the covers and innies like to burrow under them. When suitably overheated, they will work their way out to cool down. Jack Russells can be delightful companions day and night. Nothing pleases a JRT more than being right next to you, tight to your side. These dogs seem to enjoy luxury and roughing it, all in the same day.

LETTING YOUR JRT KNOW WHO'S IN CHARGE

Some terriers have a tendency to be possessive about beds. If they become grouchy about whose bed it is, it is time to be dominant and move the dog out of the bedroom. Never allow unsuitable behavior when sharing furniture with the dog. You can avoid a lot of problems by establishing rules right at the start and sticking with them.

It is always important to maintain the dog's respect. Quick to take control of the situation, JRTs can be fast to note weak humans and take advantage. They have been known to take control of beds and chairs, growling at the rightful owners. Allowed to be terrorists, they can be increasingly naughty. Possessiveness can often be diminished without confrontation by distraction. Most relish the privilege of your company, day or night. Most seek approval and affection. It is much of their charm at work or rest.

CHAPTER 8

Grooming the Jack Russell Terrier

The advantage of regular grooming is that it gives you the opportunity to look over your dog carefully and examine for ticks and other problems. It also gives you a great chance to have one-on-one time with your dog, who will enjoy the process.

The Jack Russell Terrier is not a nonshedding dog. You'll believe this when you see the dog-hair tumbleweeds of white fuzz roll across your hardwood floors daily. Keeping a pack of Jack Russell Terriers will force any respectable home manager to sweep or vacuum daily during the two major shedding periods, spring and fall. It does help to take the dogs outdoors and brush them with a stiff brush, an equine shedding blade or a rough-textured volcanic-type block used for grooming horses.

Some are convinced the smooth-coated dogs shed more than the rough- or broken-coated ones. Broken-coated simply means the dog has areas of smooth combined with a rough coat, with the smooth coat tending to appear on the ears. Conversely, the dog may appear smooth and have furnishings such as eyebrows or neck hair that are longer than smooth. Some even look smooth but have a ridge of hair along the spine. Old-timers profess the adage that one should breed smooth with broken to keep a harsh coat.

Rough-coated dogs, according to some fans of the breed, shed less than their smooth-coated brethren. It doesn't really matter which type of coat your dog has: Jack Russells shed.

The Jack Russell is a double-coated dog. The smooth type should have a dense undercoat with a harsh overcoat that will protect it from the elements and underbrush. The rough-coated Jack Russell should have a very dense undercoat with a coarse overcoat to protect it. Dogs that work below ground need a good jacket. Often they hunt in poor weather, locating earths during the fall and winter, when a good coat strongly aids their comfort.

No matter what type of coat your JRT has, this is a dog that sheds continuously. The hairs work into fabrics and can be difficult to remove. If you are uncomfortable finding sharp white hairs year-round on your clothing and furniture, and everywhere else, be warned this is unavoidable in your household. I received an emergency rescue call one evening from an excited man who wanted someone to remove the dog immediately. When I asked him what was going wrong, he declared, "He is shedding!"

I have a friend that always vacuums out his car when I have ridden in it. So many of the hairs are carried on my clothes they scatter on the car's velour interior, which drives him mad! But if you love the dog, you put up with the hair. It helps to limit the amount of dogs sharing your home if you are fastidious about something as common as dog hair. The shedding does make some people very uncomfortable. Deal patiently with the hair, or find a nonshedding breed!

Some people have a talent and patience for great turnout on horses and dogs. I have always been one that never put very pretty braids in horses, and I take the casual approach to dog grooming. Jack Russells are a working terrier and, therefore, little emphasis is put on grooming. However, it is a delight to see a well-turned-out dog. It is nice to see a dog with feet that have had the hairs trimmed so as to show the good foot, or to see a clean mouth.

CARING FOR THE COAT

Many old terriermen would simply pull their dogs' coats come spring. This is done by grasping the hair and gently pulling in the direction away from the dog to pluck out the dead hairs. It can be a timely process, and the dog may get to the point where it growls at you or runs when you have the "Let's work on your coat" look in your eye. Some folks use clippers on a very rough coat. I did a complete butchering job on a nice dog and have not picked up clippers since. My apologies to the dog to this day. Many professional dog groomers seem to carve Jack Russells into schnauzers. If all else fails, remember the dog is a working dog and not a showpiece. The coat is to help the dog be comfortable at work.

Nonetheless, a handsomely cared-for dog is a treat to behold, and there is no reason why a working dog should not look its best. The following procedure is for a thorough grooming of the terrier's coat.

Joan LaPlace deserves full credit for this list of needed supplies for making a terrier look its very best. She does an excellent job making a dog look as though every hair is in place. You will need the following supplies:

- rubber hound glove
- trimmer knife
- horsehair glove
- greyhound comb
- flea comb
- nail trimmer

Grooming a Jack Russell is not very demanding, and it's always a pleasure to encounter a well-groomed dog. (photo by Jeannie Harrison/Close Encounters of the Furry Kind)

- grooming stone (also known as a horse grooming block; feels like styrofoam)
- magnet cloth (the kind that look like chamois and absorbs a lot of water quickly)
- McClellan stripping knives, fine and coarse (these come either left- or right-handed)
- tooth scaler
- dog toothbrush and dog-specific toothpaste (or finger toothbrush for use on dog)
- thinning shears with teeth
- straight shears
- styptic powder

To work on a dog's coat, you must first place the dog on a surface that is of a height at which you can work comfortably. Your back must be comfortable for the task. Ideally, you will have a noose to restrain the dog so both hands will be free for grooming. Never leave the dog unattended while it is restrained in the noose. If you must interrupt the procedure, have a crate ready to place the dog in until you return.

It is more demanding to groom rough- or broken-coated dogs, but the finished product is also more rewarding! Comb and brush your dog to remove all the loose and dead hair. This routinely helps to keep the dirt out of the coat. There is little reason to bathe a JRT unless it rolls in something that smells just horrible, or leaves the outline of some green or brown slime in a huge patch. These dogs can find the most disgusting decomposing things to roll in and adorn themselves with!

"Stripping" Your JRT

The McClellan stripping knives work very well to remove the dead hairs that remain after brushing.

Brushing out a rough-coated dog is more work than brushing out a smooth coat—but look at the results! (photo by Winter Churchill Photography)

The object is to strip and build a "jacket" on the terrier. You may decide to run the new strippers over a brick to dull them. You never want to take off so much hair as to put a "hole" in the coat. Longer hairs are removed with the coarse stripping knife. Often the terrier carries a lot of hair growth around the neck, over the loin and on the knees. Remove only a small amount at a time. Use a straight pull, not bending your wrist, and pull in the direction in which the hair grows. Begin at the head and proceed to the neck and shoulders, then the back and thighs, ending with the sides of the dog.

When this is done, Joan refers to the dog as being in its underwear. Give the dog a break and trim the nails. Help define the foot by cutting the hair between the toes or hair that sticks out over the nails. When this is done, wait exactly ten days, and then rake out the undercoat with the trimmer

After brushing, a stripping knife will do a good job of removing dead hairs.

knife, which is used for raking and not for stripping. This instrument should be kept sharp.

When the basic coat work is done, you can go over the dog daily with the rubber hound glove and the horsehair glove. Pluck out any hairs that stick up. Every week, rake the coat to keep down excessive undercoat. If this is not done, the top coat will begin to lift and start to look untidy.

GIVING YOUR JACK RUSSELL TERRIER A BATH

Bathing the dog removes the natural oils and tends to soften the feel of the coat. The guard hairs protect the dog from thorns and scrapes. The softer undercoat functions to give warmth in cold conditions and helps cool the dog when it is warm.

Some Jack Russell Terriers enjoy swimming and water sports. Many, however, don't like to be given a bath. It is not necessary most of the time unless the dog has been skunked or has found one of those icky patches on the ground to roll in. And of course, a good reason for bathing is flea control. Make sure the dog does not get water in its ears or soap in its eyes. You can put cotton balls in the dog's ears to protect them from water. If you get soap in the dog's eyes, you can be sure it will think less of cooperating next time.

The shampoo, unless it is for flea control, should be a harsh coat preparation. Anything that contains conditioner will tend to soften the coat. The JRT is, for the most part, a rather harsh-coated dog, not linty or woolly. Wash out all soapy residue. Make sure the dog is completely dry

Just because a Jack Russell likes to swim, it doesn't mean it likes a bath. Fortunately, JRTs don't need to be bathed frequently.

before allowing it outdoors in cold weather. If you are washing an older dog, dry its coat with a hair dryer and make certain it is dry before letting the dog outside.

NAIL CARE

Nail care is important for a Jack Russell. The foot is used for digging work, and the nails should be hard and well trimmed. If you start by introducing your dog to nail trimming as a puppy, you should have no problem with maintaining its feet as an adult. I find it helps to lift up the dog completely and hold it while you trim the nails. With pups, I walk while doing this to distract them. I prefer the nail-scissor type of cutting tool to the guillotine type.

Cut the nails in good lighting so you can see the quick. You should be able to see the quick very clearly and not clip into it. If the dog has a black

Trim nails in good lighting so you can clearly see the quick.

nail, cut it back last and take off about as much as you did on the other feet. Err on the side of caution, and leave the nail a little long if you are uncertain where the quick begins. Should you nip the nail close enough to cause the dog discomfort, quickly apply styptic powder. When trimming the remaining nails, leave them a bit long so the dog does not get the idea that the nail clipping means pain.

If you are in doubt about how to trim nails, have your veterinarian show you how to do it. It is

Dogs that work below ground are susceptible to foot injuries. If your JRT pulls a nail, have your veterinarian attend to it right away.

an important task that you will want to do properly. Nails that are too long can cause the dog to stand and move incorrectly, and they can actually harm the feet.

From time to time a nail gets caught or pulled in the field. A pulled nail may be extremely painful to a terrier. Take the dog to the veterinarian for treatment if a nail is pulled and hanging, causing the dog discomfort. The pulled nail never fully grows back to its original length and harshness. Often a terrier with a history of multiple pulled nails on the front feet gets very foot-sore working below ground. It helps to keep the dog's nails trimmed on a maintained basis. The dog may never allow you to touch the "pulled" nail toe ever again! JRTs are of strong opinion.

CHAPTER 9

Showing the Jack Russell Terrier

At conformation competitions, the dogs are examined on an individual basis from head to toe and judged on how they conform to the Standard for the breed. The conformation show is held in a ring roped off for just this part of the competition. There may be more than one ring going at a time at a large gathering with more than one judge evaluating the dogs by classes.

The ring steward is the person that greets you at the gate or entrance of the ring. Have your number ready and show it to the steward so you know you are in the right class. The steward is in touch with the announcer and is busily trying to get the next class on deck to keep the show on schedule.

The judge has measurement wickets that may be used during a class if there is a question of the size of any given dog in the ring. Classes are determined by sex, size and coat. If you have any question of size, check with the steward prior to the judging so you will be in the correct class. For classification purposes, it is important for the height of your dog to be known.

Showing your dog should be fun. Relax and let your proud Jack Russell show off!

WHAT TO EXPECT IN THE RING

If you have never exhibited a dog before, don't fret; it is an easy task. It helps to watch a class or two to see what will be expected of you when you move your dog for the judge. The judge will direct you clearly. Don't be nervous; exhibiting your terrier is meant to be fun for both you and your dog. If you are edgy, your dog will sense your energies and may react badly. A relaxed owner helps the dog enjoy the experience. If you are showing a puppy, the judge will make every effort to put it at ease while looking it over with great care. No judge wants to frighten a puppy, as it may fear being handled by a stranger in the future. Most puppies are bold and friendly. The judge refrains from lifting the dog off the ground, which helps all dogs keep their confidence for the examination. The judge will approach your dog so it can see him or her, which avoids surprising or startling it.

Most judges will greet you and speak to your dog before handling the dog. Its age will be asked, as this is very important. Older dogs may show more wear and tear, and this is taken into kind consideration by the judge. Some older dogs hold up in remarkably good condition even with missing teeth and scars. As long as the scars or injuries do not interfere with the possibility of work or breeding, they do not hurt the dog in competition.

Some terrier trials have conformation competitions for spayed or neutered bitches and dogs. Unless the program for the trial lists these shows, all conformation classes are for dogs that are considered breedable stock. These trials give other exhibitors a chance to see the bitches and stud dogs and the youngsters that are being produced. Only the judge, however, has the privilege to closely examine each and every dog in the ring—trying to back-seat judge from the sidelines usually doesn't get you too far. Only the judge knows the intimate aspects of each dog, because only the judge gets to compare each one to another by handling them. The judge will line the dogs up in a uniform manner, so from the sidelines you can see the line-up from first to sixth place.

Judging the Dog's Features

After the judge hears the age of your dog, he or she will look at its eyes, the set of its ears and its

Each dog is evaluated against the breed Standard. The winning dog best meets the terms of the Standard in the eyes of the judge.

Spanning

Holding the front of the dog off the ground, the judge will then wrap his or her hands around the dog's chest. This procedure is called spanning. With this action, the judge will feel the width of the chest and then may gently compress the chest to feel for flexibility. This measurement is vital, as the chest is the key to how far the dog would be able to fit below ground in a working situation. Keep in mind that the judge is evaluating a working terrier. Although the conformation competition may be compared to the bathing suit competition in a beauty pageant, it is picking the beauty most suitable to work!

Examining the Coat

Next, the judge will more than likely ruffle the coat and feel its texture while running a hand along the spine of the dog. A good coat is a jacket that protects against the elements. The dog may have to be tightly packed in a hole in wet or cold weather, and the coat provides the only comfort it gets to bring to work. Terrier coats are made to resist weather and can be shaken to loosen dirt. Their texture makes them suitable for working below ground. The undercoat is for warmth; the overcoat, or guard hairs, help the dog resist thorns or prickers of multiflora rose, as well as burdocks and stick-a-long plants in the fall while working on the surface. Many earth entrances are in difficult-to-reach places under thorns and other unfriendly terrain.

nose. The judge will then open the mouth to examine the bite for correctness. A scissor bite is favored, but a level bite is acceptable. The judge will look at the neck of the dog and feel the angle of the scapula or shoulder blades. A nicely laid-back shoulder is sought. The judge may then lift the front half of the dog off the ground and run his or her hand down to feel the bones of the legs and look at the feet. The pads will be examined and often felt for a good foot. When standing again, the judge will look at the pasterns and observe that there are no high toes (toes that do not touch the ground). The hind feet will also be examined.

The judge will observe the amount of color on the dog. The dog must be 51 percent white or

A good coat has the right texture to protect the dog when underground. The judge will consider the texture and color of the dog's coat.

more. Its markings are of no consequence, although brindle markings are not acceptable. A Jack Russell Terrier may be completely white.

Judging the Dog's Condition

The judge may press down on the loins to see how the hocks respond, and may feel and observe the dog for its condition. The hind end of the dog will be viewed from the side to see if the stifle is of good angulation and the hocks are well let down. The pasterns in the back will be observed and the dog checked for good feet in the back. The dog should be in balance and harmony to the eye of the judge. The evaluation takes just two to three minutes!

Judging Movement

Next, the judge will ask you to move your dog so he or she can see how correctly it moves. How the judge moves the dogs may depend on the size of the ring or the size of the class. You can be sure the judge is observing each dog as it comes in the ring. The judge may look up at any given time and visually compare the dog being handled with one that has been examined. It is wise to be relaxed (to a degree) but on your toes if the judge is looking. There is no need to tire a dog by asking it to hold itself nicely and proudly while each and every dog is being examined. The judge will ask you to move away in a straight line or to make a triangle. This allows the judge to look at the dog's movement going away, from the side, and approaching.

A nice, fluid movement is sought. The dog should move effortlessly with reach in front and drive from behind. The movement should not be jerky. The gait should be relaxed. Never hold the leash too tightly and string the dog up; this interferes with the natural movement of the dog. It is best to move a dog on a loose leash. Don't allow your dog to get too near another in the ring. This makes a terrible distraction and may cause a fight to break out! The dog may be ill at ease with the situation and find any excuse to blow off a little steam in terrier style.

AND THE WINNER IS. . .

When all dogs have been examined on an individual basis, the judge will look at them again as a group, and may ask them to move around the ring

Foxwarren Floyd, pictured here, was clearly a strong competitor in the show ring.

one time or keep going as the top choices are called into the center of the ring. Pay attention, as a simple wave of the hand may direct you to the center.

Good sportsmanship is appreciated by the judge. Groaning or complaining about the placing of your dog is not looked upon favorably. Your dog may place better or worse at the next terrier trial. It may improve in condition or fare differently in a different competition. The judge may be faced with many wonderful correct dogs that could be highly placed. It does seem that only one person is happy about the results, and that is the winner. As a judge, it is nice to see the smile on the last-placed exhibitor and a polite manner from those excused from the ring.

SHOWING TIPS

Some dogs love to be shown and some would rather not be. There are those that will ham it up and go in the ring with poise and grace. Others seem to think something is going to happen to them and just don't care for the lack of action of the conformation ring. No stacking is ever done. It is fine to bring something the dog likes to eat to get it to pay attention to you.

Do not use a squeaky toy excessively, or you may be excused from the ring for being a distraction. Sometimes a dog will show plenty of attention just knowing you have some goody in your pocket. Others will require more work to show them off. Sometimes your dog will pay attention to the exhibitor in front of you and look magnificent for that person (and just great for being judged)! Sometimes, at just the wrong minute, your dog will sit down or wilt, or cock a leg. All this goes with showing terriers and should be taken in stride. Judges can see deeper than a pretty pose.

CHAPTER 10

Hunting, Performance Activities and Other Fun Things

Owners of Jack Russell Terriers have many options when it comes to doing things with their dogs, from formal competitions to fun and games. And it's a good thing, too, because Jack Russells have so much energy and *joie de vivre* that sports rank high on their list of favorite things.

Any animal living a life of doing what it was bred to do has the chance at the highest form of purpose and, consequently, joy. When the relationship between dogs and humankind is based on communication, compassion and purpose, this joy is achievable for both. Today's Jack Russell Terrier owners should strive to bring this kind of joy to their dog's life by understanding its innate desire to work.

TERRIER COMPETITIONS

Jack Russell Terrier owners are fortunate to have many sanctioned terrier trials to attend each year. The JRTCA sponsors regional trials and a national trial. Over 800 dogs have attended past national trials. The annual meeting of the Jack Russell Terrier Club of America is held at the national trial.

JRT trials give terrier owners a chance to meet and talk. People often bring along tailgate picnics and share lunches with each other. Frequently, a seminar is given to help owners learn more about the Jack Russell Terrier. Bad weather does not stop a terrier trial. The event will be held in pouring rain, blowing snow, deep mud or heat over 100 degrees.

JRTCA-sanctioned Jack Russell Terrier competitions must include conformation and go-to-ground competitions. Racing may be included, and usually is. Trailing and locating is sometimes offered, as are Obedience and Agility competitions. All of these events are discussed in this chapter except conformation, which is detailed in Chapter 9. There may be a ball toss, water races, or even a costume class just for fun. With all the events offered, it is likely that your dog will take to and excel at many disciplines offered at a sanctioned trial.

With the recognition of the Jack Russell Terrier by the American Kennel Club on January 1, 1998, JRTs may now compete in several AKC-sponsored events, including Tracking Trials, Earthdog Tests (the JRT favorite!), Agility Contests and Obedience Trials, and they may also compete in Canine Good Citizen programs.

Remember to pack food and water for the dogs to take along to the competition. Be prepared to honor the judge's decision, as the decision of

Many competitions sanctioned by the JRTCA include dog races.

the judge in each division is final. At JRTCA events, dogs other than Jack Russell Terriers may not be welcomed on the grounds, but this decision is made by the trial chairman. The dogs are excited and bark as it is. They arrive ready for action and participation. The appearance of a dog of another breed can turn the trial site into a barkathon! All the rules of the trial are printed in the trial flyer that contains the entry form.

Go-to-Ground

One of the things Jack Russells can learn to do is travel through a system of tunnels to a caged rat. At JRTCA competitions this activity is called "go-to-ground." I think it is fair to say this concept was created by Pat Adams Lent, who founded the American Working Terrier Association in 1971. The principle is to encourage the dog to enter an artificial earth and "work" the caged rat—lunging, growling or barking. In JRTCA go-to-ground competition, staring at the rat is also considered working. This doesn't harm or even seem to bother the rats; in fact, in some competitions I've seen the rats sleep through the encounters.

A caged rat is the quarry in go-to-ground competitions.

The important lesson to the dog and handler in the go-to-ground event is to develop communication as a team. The purpose is to develop the team's confidence to go into natural situations and attempt to locate game below ground. It can be very frightening to see one's beloved pet vanish into the earth out of sight. It can also be a delight to hear the dog bark at whatever is holed in, doing what it is bred to do. The grounds for good earth work are based in obedience and communication. Nothing is more satisfying than asking a dog to work, seeing it respond to the handler and having it all come together as teamwork.

In the Novice classes, safely caged rats are at the end of a ten-foot tunnel with one turn. In the Open and Certificate competitions, the dogs race to the caged rats through a tunnel with two bends. There is an advanced Certificate class offered at some trials with a tunnel that is a minimum of forty feet with four 90-degree turns. This is called a super earth. It is the biggest challenge to the certificate dogs. It requires more problem solving for the dog and, although completely safe, is a little more like the challenge of working below ground. Some super earths have multiple openings, but only one leads to the underground network leading to the quarry. The dog has a set amount of time to enter and complete the maze.

Handler and dog must work together as a team in go-to-ground competitions. This is a great way to learn to communicate with your Jack Russell.

Certificate dogs have successfully completed both the Novice and Open classes. Any dog that has successfully completed the Open class cannot enter the Novice or Open class again. Terriers that have earned a score of 100 percent in an Open Go-to-Ground class within the last 30 days, and terriers that have turned 1 year of age within the last 30 days, upon proof of age, may enter the Certificate Go-to-Ground by showing a 100-percent Open score sheet to the den steward. The den steward assists the judge in organizing the event and keeping the entries in order.

Each dog is judged in the same manner: by the amount of time it takes to locate the rat. Competitions can be won by a hundredth of a second. The quality of the marking of the rats may determine placement if dogs have the same times. This, however, is rare.

At every competition, the rats are treated humanely by the judge and staff. It is not the point to inflict any harm on the rats; they remain safely caged all day and are removed from the grounds after the last dog competes. During the competition it is mandatory that the rats have clean bedding, food and fresh water available at all times.

The dog must pass the time constraints and working requirements to receive a placement based on the fastest time. Schooling prior to the competition with the tunnels on site is not permitted. Exhibitors are expected to pick up their score

The winning dog in a go-to-ground competition is the one that locates the rat most quickly.

sheets for their terriers at the secretary's stand and, at the time of the competition, to take them to the den steward for scoring by the judge. Your dog's number will be in your entry packet if you preregistered; you will be given a number at the event if you post-enter.

The score sheet contains important information regarding the requirements, specifications and judging criteria of each class. The go-to-ground starts when the terrier is released, so that all four of the dog's feet are on the ground before crossing the starting line. This is an important rule. After you release your dog, you stand by the entrance hole. You can talk to or command your dog with encouragement any time during its turn to compete. The judge will tell you when to go to the catch area (behind the barricade of hay), at which time you pick up your dog and are finished with the event.

Similar competitions sponsored by the American Kennel Club are known as Earthdog Tests, which provide an opportunity for the dog to display its ability to follow game and work quarry. In these events, the quarry is either live (such as two caged rats) or artificial (scented so as to attract the dogs).

Dogs advance through four levels of achievement in Earthdog Tests. A dog receives no qualifications or titles from competing in the beginner's Introduction to Quarry event, but has an opportunity to enter a den and scent the quarry. After passing this level, dogs compete for Junior Earthdog, Senior Earthdog and finally Master Earthdog titles. At each level the dog is asked to display a greater degree of skill in locating and tracking a scent, and in negotiating increasingly complex dens and tunnels.

And they're off!

Of course, other breeds of terriers will also be competing at Earthdog Trials.

Racing

The high-powered, active Jack Russell Terrier loves racing. By simply entering your dog in races it will learn from participating, but it is wiser to do some training at home first.

First, purchase a basket muzzle that fits your dog properly. The basket muzzle allows the dog to open its mouth and pant. The reason for racing in a muzzle is safety. During a race the terriers make a sprint down a course that is a minimum of 150 feet long, which gets the blood up and the heart beating. At the finish line, the object of the chase vanishes and the dogs are inclined to pitch into each other. The muzzle prevents any serious fighting, prevents an overexcited dog from nipping the handler that scoops it up at the finish and prevents any dog from tearing at the lure. Fighting in a race is grounds for elimination.

It is easy to get a dog accustomed to a muzzle. At first you just slip it on and play with the dog or distract it so it is not compelled to take it off. If it is properly adjusted, it will be hard for the dog to

Muzzles are worn by the racers for safety purposes—racing gets the dogs very excited and they may get nippy with their handler, or each other.

remove. Note a dog that takes its muzzle off during a race is eliminated. The muzzle training sessions should be short and sweet. Reward the dog for accepting the muzzle with a treat. Later, the muzzle will bring a fond racing memory to the dog, and it will not object when you put it on.

Each dog wears a racing collar of a different color for ease of spotting. It is important to note that the finish line is behind a barrier made of straw or hay bales with a hole in it that is about eight inches square. Ideally only one dog can come through the tunnel at a time. This simulates a situation in which the chased "quarry" has gone to ground and vanished. The dog must follow the lure, which is the quarry, through the hole and into its "den."

Sometimes one dog will push another aside at the bale and come through with more force and

win. JRTs are motivated to catch the lure! The lure is often scented to make the chase more interesting to the dogs, and it is run with a crank device. There is a finish-line judge that verifies the placement of the racing dogs.

Many a fast dog has lost a race by not going through the barrier. Teaching your dog to run through a barrier is something you can do at home. Set up some bales or whatever may be safe with an opening. Put a toy or an old sock on a string and get the dog to chase it through the barrier. This is good training to prepare your dog for a competitive race.

You can further train your dog for racing by shaking the lure and excitedly saying "get it." Jack Russells catch on quickly that this is a good game and will want to get the lure. In a real race, if the lure is caught, the race needs to be rerun. In training, the dog may enjoy catching the lure and being very satisfied with itself. Winning the lure makes the training more fun for the dog!

There are flat races and hurdle races. The hurdle races have jumps placed along the race course that are of appropriate height to the age of the dog. Puppies are asked to make smaller jumps than adult dogs. The low hurdles are up to eight inches high, and the higher hurdles are over eight inches. Races are set up with safety in mind. Sometimes the little dogs put in a bad jump and tumble. Some recover and still place well by the finish line. The races are lots of fun for both the dogs and all who watch.

Not all dogs like to race. Some feel overwhelmed at the excitement of the other dogs and

Look at these dogs go for the water jump! They are having the time of their lives!

the crowds of spectators. Other terriers absolutely love to race. I had a dog that would roll in her crate in an apparent effort to speed herself to the racecourse. Mild at home, she was a maniac when it came to racing. I think she liked to hear her name over the loudspeaker when she placed. If your dog does not like to race, you're sure to find something else it will enjoy.

Here are some of the basic racing rules for JRTCA-sanctioned trials that participants need to know. All dogs must be muzzled. Plastic basket muzzles are strongly suggested; no figure-eight

muzzles are allowed. Any terrier entering the catch area during a race without a secured muzzle will be disqualified. Handlers should have their entries prepared to race, be aware of their classes and be ready when called. The order in which entries are placed in the starting box is determined by drawing numbers for positions. Once entries are loaded into the starting gate, all handlers shall proceed to the finish line and be ready to receive their terrier.

Any entry starting a fight will be disqualified by the racing judge from further racing that day. In a hurdle race, any entry going around the jumps will be disqualified. If a brush or lure is caught, the race will be rerun. Entries must cross the finish line completely to place in a race; the finish line is the back side of the barrier. Racing Champion is determined by a runoff of first-place terriers in each class in each division.

Obedience Trials

Those of us dedicated to the Jack Russell Terrier know that to put the words *obedience* and *Jack Russell Terrier* in the same sentence is a giggle. If the Jack Russell *likes* obedience and wants to please you by doing it cleanly, you will be richly rewarded with a new level of communication.

Obedience has nothing to do with having dominance over the dog. It refers to training a dog

High hurdles are for adult dogs.

to perform a set of exercises—everything from long sits and downs to retrieving over jumps and scent discrimination—that are scored by a judge. The dog must find obedience meaningful and fun or it will never succeed. You can never hammer a JRT into being a brilliant obedience performer. These dogs are too intelligent and too much themselves to ever be little robots. The ones that perform well give me goose bumps, because it means their handlers are fun, brave, and persevering. I have the utmost respect for those who train their dogs to off-lead obedience in a performance that is sunny and eager the entire time.

I still am amused by the memory of my favorite dog, Nester Acorn, who took rather readily to obedience. He wanted nothing more than to please me, unless he was hunting, which was a

game all on his terms. We were practicing the exercise of heeling in a figure-eight around the human "poles." When I set off in the wrong direction my trainer immediately said, "No, no, no!" Nester heard her and simply fell to the ground on his side. It brought the entire class to a standstill in a fit of laughter. Nester's daughter, Zenith Acorn, who loves hunting and go-to-ground, held the long down to within seconds of achievement, then suddenly sprang up to run to the go-to-ground area to take another turn.

Obedience is basic training that makes for much better understanding between man and beast. It is very good to have the dog learn to mind and respect you. It is a valuable lesson for the dog to learn to pay complete attention to you. An obedience-trained dog will stay in the car waiting when you unload groceries, or will learn not to storm through a door just because it is opened. Guests will be able to come to your house to find a dog that is sitting and not bouncing off the walls to greet them.

If you hunt your terrier, the recall learned in obedience training may save you hours of digging for a headstrong out-of-control dog or hours of searching for your missing dog deep in the woods. The recall and stay are the best commands you can teach your dog. Both could potentially save the dog's life.

At a JRTCA Obedience Trial, classes are limited in size. To earn a qualifying score, the terrier needs to earn 170 out of 200 points and receive no less than 50 percent of any points given for each exercise. Half-points may be used to determine a qualifying score. Any terrier receiving three qualifying scores in the same class, under two different judges, is eligible for a JRTCA Obedience Certificate; the terrier must be JRTCA registered or recorded, and the owner must be a current member of the JRTCA. The certificate may be obtained by submitting signed score sheets along with the appropriate fee to the JRTCA.

Jack Russells may also compete in Obedience Trials sponsored by the American Kennel Club. AKC competition is conducted in three levels, with each level requiring the performance of increasingly difficult exercises. To obtain a Novice–Companion Dog title, the dog must show its ability to respond to basic commands. The second level, completion of which earns a dog an Open–Companion Dog Excellent title, demands that the dog perform off-leash and for longer periods of time. It also entails jumping and retrieving skills. Finally, the Utility–Utility Dog title requires the dog to perform even more demanding exercises and to demonstrate scent discrimination abilities. A dog need not be of "show-dog" quality to compete—any purebred dog over three months of age that is registered with the organization may enter.

Agility Trials

An Agility Trial is one of the best activities for the Jack Russell who needs a sport that leads to happiness and harmony. Agility is fun for both terriers and owners. It builds great communication between the dog and handler. For those people

Agility Trials are a fun way to communicate and bond with your JRT.

who choose to give their dog a challenge that is both safe and a great outlet for the dog's seemingly endless energy level, agility is an excellent activity. Keep in mind there are brilliant hunting dogs that also shine at agility.

Agility Trials are modeled on equestrian stadium jumping. There are all sorts of jumps and obstacles that form a course over which dog and handler must navigate. Agility contests first appeared as entertainment at the Crufts Dog Show in England in 1979, and the sport has been growing in popularity ever since. There are now several national organizations for agility, which have established rules and specifications. These include the American Kennel Club (AKC), the United States Dog Agility Association (USDAA) and the National Club for Dog Agility (NCDA).

In an Agility Trial, the dog navigates through a series of obstacles and jumps.

In Agility Trials, the handler has a set amount of time to direct a dog off-leash through an obstacle course. Handlers can give as many commands or visual signals to their dog as necessary, but in competition you may not touch the dog or the equipment. There are faults for knocking obstacles down or not placing one or more feet in the contact or safety zone when ascending or descending certain pieces of equipment. If the obstacles are taken out of sequence, or if the dog goes past or stops before the next obstacle, there are faults assigned. Time penalties are also assigned for exceeding the "Standard Course Time" or "SCT." The dog with the fewest faults and the best time is the winner.

The obstacles are arranged in various configurations that are unique each time they are assembled by the judge for a competition. The level of difficulty is appropriate to the experience and level of ability. As the team of dog and handler move successfully to higher levels, the course becomes more complex and challenging. Time and accuracy are of the essence.

Jack Russell Terriers, being very athletic, shine at this discipline. Because agility is something most dogs enjoy, they learn quickly. Training can begin with young dogs, but organizations have a minimum age requirement for participation. The dog needs to be mentally and physically mature enough to be up to the rigors of agility.

Agility promotes confidence in a dog and a spirit of teamwork with the handler. It is based on positive encouragement, which is wonderful for dogs. The vocabulary and signals increase as the team fine-tunes to compete successfully. Even at a full tilt, the dog must be willing to understand and respond to the handler for accuracy. Split-second timing may make a big difference in the outcome of competition.

Agility is a competition that is inspiring to watch. As with obedience, the level of communication that is developed between handler and dog can be applied elsewhere. All such learning makes living with a dog more enjoyable and successful. All dogs must be one year old or older to compete in any Agility class, and should be fit and up to the task, along with the handler! Some of the happiest-looking dogs are those doing the highest level of agility. You can find local agility clubs in your area that can get you and your dog started in this super-fun activity.

"The table," where a dog needs to stop and stay during the middle of its agility routine, is undoubtedly the most difficult "obstacle" for the Jack Russell. This dog manages nicely.

HUNTING AND THE JACK RUSSELL TERRIER

In England, the Jack Russell Terrier was developed to be a part of the pest-control process. The pest was often a fox that had raided a farmer's chicken coops or barns, making off with chickens or lambs. Often a farmer would enlist a local who kept a few game terriers to find the den of the offending fox. The dog would locate the fox and go to earth to find it. Arriving on the scene, the JRT's handler would dig to locate the dog, which would be baying face-to-face with the fox. The handler of the dog managed the harvest or relocation of the offending fox. The JRT was *not* developed to harm the fox.

Jack Russell Terriers have also been used in conjunction with packs of fox-hounds in England and, briefly, in the United States. The terrier is much smaller than the foxhounds and generally cannot keep up with them when they are in full pursuit. The terrier learns shortcuts to dens and knows the country well, or it rides with its owner or handler in a specially designed saddlebag. Often the terrier will anticipate where the hounds will put the fox to ground and get there to dive in the earth. Once in the earth the little dog, with the sheer force of its instincts, tries to dislodge the fox so that it moves back to the surface and out again. All the dog has is its voice and overwhelming presence of will against the denned fox, and often that is enough to make the fox exit from a hole.

Often a bolted fox, unharmed but curious, will pause at the surface a small distance off and glance back in wonder. The terrier may not surface immediately after the fox. This gives the fox the opportunity to trot off unruffled by the exchange, though some choose to get out at full speed.

Always let the dog enter the opening of any earth using its mind, nose and instincts. Do not

Practicing—maneuvering over the obstacles with your Jack Russell on-lead—helps to develop your skills as an agility team.

cheer on a dog with foolhardy handler enthusiasm. Stay calm and allow the dog to make the choice. Be patient. Nothing reveals an amateur hunter more than cheerleading at an earthen entrance. Getting a dog fired up and too keen is risking sending it full bore into a big annoyed critter. Let the dog hunt. The dog may be encouraged by your presence and patience. A senior dog can be an excellent teacher by example and can help with young or inexperienced dogs.

Each state has specific game laws, and it may be illegal to put a dog in an earth in your state. It is important to familiarize yourself with the game laws of each state. If you work your terrier, you may be required by law to obtain a hunting license. The funding from the license supports game conservation. Always keep current on the legal aspects of hunting in your state.

Hunting is defined in the *New York State Hunting and Trapping Regulation Guide, 1996–1997* edition, as "to pursue, shoot, hunt, kill or capture (other than trap) wildlife and includes all lesser acts

EFFICIENT BARN DOGS

Jack Russells are often kept around stables and barns to control rodent populations that enjoy these environments due to the easy availability of grain and other foods. The little dog often makes a big job of ferreting out unwanted invaders to grain bins and hay lofts of country barns and stables.

A JRT will patrol to find and destroy the unwanted invaders. A good barn-hunting terrier may spend hours focused on an area where the scent indicates the path of a rodent. A Jack Russell Terrier has the ability to spring like a fox or cat and catch the rodent. Many a good terrier silently bursts into a barn before its slower human companion and zips to its favorite site to work on hunting a pesky rat or mouse.

that disturb, harry or worry wildlife whether or not they result in taking or attempting to take the animal." Encountering wildlife while accompanied by terriers falls under this regulation and requires a hunting license. I feel that unless one has a pest control problem or is attempting to feed oneself or one's family with game, there is no reason to harm any quarry encountered. It is in the best interest of preservation of good hunting to always be humane.

One of the most important considerations when taking a dog to the field to work is the possibility of losing the dog. JRTs can work their way deeply into the earth and get trapped below ground. Sometimes soil conditions create cave-ins. Most dogs will try their hardest to get out, but it is a fact that some never surface again. A dog may lack oxygen or go into shock below ground. If quarry blocks the exit and a battle takes place, the dog cannot always get out. In the excited process of digging, many dogs have basically buried themselves alive.

Some hunters carry their terriers in a saddlebag designed especially for the dog.

It is very frightening to have a dog perish below ground. If you go out hunting with your terrier, make sure you have friends you can call if you need help. Know where the nearest backhoe is. Earth dens may be dangerous, and rock dens even more so, because there are tons of stone between the handler and the dog. Make sure you can be of help to your dog if the going gets tough. Do not allow two dogs to enter a den at once. The dog behind may push the dog in front into a situation where it cannot back up to duck and dodge harm.

Terriers Afield

Terriers in the field have some serious foes: skunks, porcupines and poisonous snakes, to name a few. Insect stings can bring on allergic reactions in some dogs, and multiple stings may cause a dog to go into shock. *Bufo* toads are found throughout the United States, and many members of this frog family emit a dangerous toxin. If a dog picks one up with its mouth, the toxin can enter its bloodstream and be fatal. In

Most hunters engage in the hunt for sport—they do not harm their quarry.

You and your Jack Russell are a team in the field. It's a great way to bond with your dog.

some areas of the United States there are badgers, the most formidable animal the JRT may meet.

Skunks

Skunks appeal to Jack Russell Terriers. The scent of the red fox is likened to sweet-smelling skunk odor. Many terriers will eagerly enter a hole that holds a skunk. It is an exceptional dog that will come when it is called and leave a skunk alone. The risk of death to a dog sprayed below ground is very real. If the skunk sprays the dog in the face below ground in close quarters, the spray can enter its lungs and inhibit its ability to breathe.

Many terriers are lost to skunks. The dog may go into anaphylactic shock as a reaction to the spraying. Some veterinarians can save a dog sprayed by a skunk by placing it on oxygen and treating it immediately. Call ahead to let the veterinarian know you are bringing in a dog that has been skunked below ground so the office is prepared to treat your dog. Do not waste any time getting the dog to help.

A dog that has been sprayed by a skunk *stinks!* The smell is difficult to get off the dog, and may also cling to the collar, leash or you. Almost everyone has a remedy for getting rid of the smell. One recipe that has worked for me was provided by Kirk Dixon and Mike Bilbo. They use 1 quart of hydrogen peroxide (3 percent), mixed with 1 cup of baking soda and 1 tablespoon of dishwashing detergent.

Porcupines

Porcupines are another animal to try to avoid. The porcupine has from 15,000 to 30,000 quills that can be up to four inches long. Porcupines turn their hindquarters to their attackers, then quickly move sideways and backwards to attack, ramming the quills into the predator. (It is not true that porcupines can aim and shoot their spikes at an enemy.) A warning sign of porcupines in the area will be damaged bark at the base of trees. Like the beaver, the porcupine's teeth continuously grow and must be trimmed frequently by chewing on bark.

A word of advice: Porcupine attacks can be deadly. If your dog is quilled, seek veterinary attention immediately. The quills are very painful to extract and the dog should be sedated during the procedure. Try not to let your Jack Russell Terrier paw or bite at the quills in transport. When a quill breaks, it is much more difficult to retrieve. Jack Russells are smart dogs, but when they smell vermin they go after it every time.

There are numerous dangers to Jack Russells afield. In addition to becoming trapped in the earth, a dog can be attacked by wildlife. Be prepared to help your JRT in an emergency.

Coyotes

Coyotes are yet another grave danger to the Jack Russell Terrier. I have heard of coyotes that have enticed a terrier to play and then taken the dog away, leaving no trace, not even a tuft of coat. Coyotes prefer easy and accessible prey. According to the Department of Environmental Conservation's wildlife technician, Jim Eckler, "Coyotes will eat just about anything they can find. The coyote eats small game down to snakes, frogs, and insects. When game is scarce they eat fruit, berries, insects, corn, and even garbage."

Although a private animal, the coyote can be spotted running swales in fields. A swale is a low-lying indentation in the natural lay of the land. Coyotes will leave markings of urine and scat near the edges of their territory. I have discovered such an area on our farm.

The Hunting Kit

Before going into the field with a hunting dog, most people put together a collection of items they may need. Some carry elaborate kits with medical supplies, others a simple waist pouch with just a few items. What to carry can also change with the seasons.

Kirk Dixon and Mike Bilbo have been instrumental in creating this list of tools needed for successful earthwork. Anyone may develop a shortened version of their own kit for earthwork during different seasons under different conditions.

This list includes a range of items tested through experience.

- Tracking collar and receiver
- Extra batteries for both collar and box
- Electrical tape for wrapping the collar transmitter
- Cellular phone
- Stake to tie extra terriers when digging
- Water bottle and dish
- Eye wash for cleaning soil from the dog's eyes
- Insect repellent for summertime
- Hand-warmer packets for inside mittens or socks in winter
- Wire cutters
- Shovels, both long- and short-handled
- Post hole digger
- Saw for roots
- Digging bar and pick
- Bucket to remove dirt in deep digs
- Flashlight

Items to have nearby if needed include a chainsaw; a snare; rubber gloves; a change of clothes appropriate for conditions; blankets and towels; back-up flashlights or a lantern; a bottle of skunk odor remover; and a predator call, party favor or fawn bleat (making odd noises can urge a

Some of the items you should bring along for the hunt.

dog to come to a handler when calling fails). Include a complete first aid kit equipped for man and beast.

The first aid kit should include eye wash, antibiotic ointment, betadine solution, gauze and bandages, surgical tape and tweezers. An eye wash made of a boric acid solution (boric acid can be purchased at any drugstore) is suggested. The solution is inexpensive and can also be used to wash out wounds. It is gentle to the eyes and can prevent swelling the day after work below ground. Include the phone numbers of local veterinarians in case of an emergency. Keeping some high-energy food on hand may help tired earth workers.

Other Precautions

In addition to having the appropriate tools, there are other considerations when setting off to hunt. It is always advised to note the wind direction. By keeping the wind in your face when casting your terriers to work, your scent, which gives warning of your presence in the woods, is not traveling ahead of you. Always work your terriers quietly. Do not chatter or be noisy in the woods or fields. Never litter or leave gates open. Always have permission of the landowner to be on his or her land. If you dig a hole, always close it when you are finished digging. Good conduct in the field is always correct and considerate.

No dog should be allowed to enter the earth without a locator collar. The collar has a receiver, and the box is a transmitter so a dog can be located below ground. Batteries should be changed frequently and the collar examined for wear prior to earth work. Using a locator collar can be critical to saving your dog's life should there be a problem below ground. It can be hard to guess the location of a dog barking below ground. The twists and turns of the sett may make the sounds below deceptive and difficult to read for locating the dog. Because it is desirable to dig to a working dog that has settled into work, it is vital to know where the dog is.

Always let someone know exactly where you are going and when you expect to be back. If you have one, bring a portable phone with you, and always carry a whistle in case you or your dog suffers a physical injury while in the field. When you don't return on schedule and someone comes looking for you, a whistle will outlast your voice and carry farther. Dogs have even been known to respond to a whistle, so it can serve two important functions.

Never ask a dog that has not first had a good meal early in the day to work. Feed the dog well upon getting home—your Jack Russell should have worked up an appetite and if it does not want to eat, concern is appropriate. Wear rubber gloves to handle a dog when washing it off after working. Check the mouth for injury from pulling roots or from bites if contact has been made with any quarry. You may have to remove dirt that is packed in the roof of the dog's mouth. The dog may also have been bitten in its mouth. The gloves will offer you protection from rabies. Check the dog entirely from head to toe for any injuries.

There is no way of knowing the health of the undomesticated animal in any given hole. Sometimes animals will earth up as their health fails. Mange, for example, will weaken an animal. Rabies causes abnormal behavior and is fatal. It takes only the swipe of infected saliva across a cut to introduce the fatal virus to the system. Dogs are routinely protected by rabies as a condition of obtaining a dog license, but very few people seek the protection of pre-exposure inoculations. Keep the dog's rabies protection current. Guard yourself very carefully from exposure to rabies. Avoid any animal you encounter in the wild that is not behaving in a normal manner.

Teaching a Dog to Hunt

Teaching a terrier to hunt is often a matter of exposure. It is always good to let a young dog learn by observing a senior working dog. The instinct to enter an earthen tunnel is very strong in the Jack Russell Terrier. Encourage an inexperienced dog to go in safe holes in open fields. Many will pick up on a scent around the hole and want to investigate. You can sit quietly and allow the dog to "play."

The time will come when your JRT meets the resident of the hole. Expect the dog either to be a bit insecure or to bay. A lot of good dogs start slowly and become excellent workers. It takes patience for a young dog to successfully learn to be a reliable hunting dog. Early barks and interest in work should be encouraged. Protect the dog from any adverse experiences if at all possible. A dog that is frightened or hurt when learning either reacts by being shy or getting intent on working

the opponent in the ground. Many people allow a younger or inexperienced dog to meet quarry in a protected way. As a rule, it does not take long for the dog to understand what to do.

It is sometimes best to begin hunting as an observer—take your dog along on a leash, so it can watch too! You can help by carrying shovels or any backpacks with supplies. You may take a turn digging and taking direction from those more experienced. Both you and your dog can learn from the exposure of just being along. In case of any problems, it is good to have accomplished handlers there for guidance.

Hard and Soft Dogs

Different dogs have different styles of working. The Jack Russell Terrier has been bred to locate and bay at the presence of an earth-dwelling animal. Some terriers will be able to influence the animal to leave by forcing its will with its mere presence. A "soft" terrier may lunge at or gently nip at the animal it is working without combat. A "hard" terrier is one that is more aggressive or combative in style, perhaps having built up an attitude from previous experiences. There are situations where a "hard" dog is useful. Some dogs are "hard" by nature, which is reflected in their style of working.

Cindy O'Reilly, a JRTCA working judge, wrote the poem on the next page, which sums up the situation best:

Working with another dog is a good way for a terrier to learn the tricks of the trade.

THE HARD ONE

The hard dog's the one that breaks your heart,
He always comes out ripped apart.
He's the first in line when you load the collars,
As you drive away you can still hear his hollers.
You just can't pay to patch him up again,
His face already wears a permanent grin.
He's missing way too much skin by now,
But he really wants to hunt somehow.

Hunting has always been his passion,
You just can't afford his working fashion.
So you let him rid the basement of mice,
It's work for him at an affordable price.
You bless the soft dog that has taken his place,
You know when he comes out he'll still have his face.
You may lose some quarry with the soft one's bays,
But at least you can hunt him for the rest of his days.

CHAPTER 11

The Behavior and Training of Your Jack Russell Terrier

BEHAVIOR

Hunting with a dog is not everybody's cup of tea. Some people just don't want to risk losing their dog, and some are not interested in chasing wild animals. However, the instinct to work remains in the dog regardless. Keeping a dog away from work may cause other behaviors (invariably undesirable ones) to amplify as a result of not working. Exercise will keep the pet dog on an even keel. *Lots* of exercise is needed.

Never bore a Jack Russell Terrier. When left alone, these dogs have been known to engage in activities that people find shocking. One man arrived home to his apartment to find the place torn apart. He called the police, but by the time they arrived he had figured out that his brace of Jack Russells was responsible for the "break-in."

When left alone all day, some JRTs become very vocal. Some decide to chew or dig. Some mark or soil the place. A JRT wants to be with you as much as possible. Clearly, it has an opinion on what it wants to do.

Some Jack Russells decide when their people are a bit dull that they need to take over the leadership of the home. It seems to start innocently enough. The dog takes over the couch, then the bed. Some people find they are not allowed to use these pieces of furniture without the dog protesting. As amusing as it may sound, the twelve-pound dog may end up ruling the roost! Accordingly, a Jack Russell needs leadership. Most are very relieved to be given direction and stop dominant behavior if corrected consistently and firmly. Remember, however, one must never be unjust in punishment; it is not necessary to strike a JRT to get a point across. The dogs' intelligence allows a great range of communication that never warrants a heavy hand.

Most Jack Russells are cheerful and willing to please. They can spot who does not want their attention and will continue to try to win that person over. They will play hard and be assertive in their play. Clearly they want to win any game of tug of war. If you play ball with them, the ball will

The tireless JRT likes to play—and likes to win.

always be in their court. They like winning and never get tired of it.

Jack Russells play very hard with each other. When they have a buddy they will play for endless hours together. On the other hand, if they have an enemy, there is no peace from that war. It is strongly advised to keep no more than two dogs together unattended or in a yard. If there is a disagreement, it is ugly, sometimes a fight to the death. If two dogs decide that they do not like each other and square off fighting a few times, one will probably have to find a new home. The battle will never end. There may be peaceful times, but another fight will eventually erupt.

It is accurate to say the Jack Russell Terrier is assertive. It is considered a fault for the dog to be either too shy or too aggressive. This is a not a back-burner dog nobody will know is present—it demands to be noticed. The biggest insult you can heap upon a Jack Russell is to ignore it. About 90 percent of the behavior problems of this dog stem from lack of physical or mental activity. You will not be able to compromise the very real needs of this dynamic dog.

On the other hand, you should not encourage any overly assertive behavior, and a young puppy will often need training to moderate this attribute. One way to do this is to put the young pup on your lap, face it belly-up and constrict its activity until it settles.

While assertive conduct should be kept in check, overly submissive behavior is also considered problematic. When you understand submissiveness, you can correct it gently. A submissive dog often will greet a human member of its pack by urinating. Owners are often bewildered by this behavior, which in canine behavior is meant to be a compliment.

To help the dog feel less submissive, be careful not to give body signals that are dominant. Leaning over a small dog, an action that we perceive to be a innocuous, is read as domination by the animal. Try exercises where you sit at the dog's level and have the dog come to you. Allow the dog to take the initiative and avoid making a number of voice or hand signals. Encourage play that allows the dog to be a winner. A gentle game of tug of war where the dog wins may help build confidence. When greeting the dog, tone down the greeting by entering the house without making eye contact with, talking to or touching the dog. Allow the dog outside and, when it relieves itself in an appropriate manner, speak to it with controlled measured praise. Do not use an excited voice.

TRAINING

Many movies, television shows and commercials feature the Jack Russell Terrier. Part of this media exposure is due to the popularity of this cute little comedian. Another reason may be because these dogs can be trained to act. The bright mind and agile body of the JRT make for a good subject.

Training a JRT is based on communication and reward. No one can force a Jack Russell Terrier into doing anything, so it's up to you to make any training worthy of the dog. When the dog can decipher that there is something in it that's of interest, you may get results, but don't count on it. Much of the charm of relating to the Jack Russell is knowing the terms of the relationship are never carved in stone.

The most important lesson to teach any dog is to come when called. Start when the dog is a puppy. Reinforce any recall with untiring praise and food as a reward. This means having a bit of kibble or biscuit in your pocket anytime you're out with your puppy. Over time, you can begin to provide random food rewards, giving the dog a snack only every third time it comes, but never stop giving praise. Some Jack Russell Terriers will do anything to please their pet person and willingly perform tasks.

Distracting a JRT works well in many situations. You may have a split second to catch the attention of your dog before it bolts to some action you would rather avoid. Get its attention with excited chatter, or march off in a different direction with great purpose. A good way to catch a naughty young dog that does not want to come to you is to open a car door. Most love to ride in the car and will hop right in. Teach a JRT to wait for your signal and not beat you through a door.

Housetraining

Housetraining a Jack Russell presents a challenge to many owners. It is wrong to expect much until the dog is about four months old, and sometimes older. The puppy cannot control its body functions until about this age.

For housetraining to succeed, it's important to establish and stick to a schedule. As soon as the pup wakes and soon after eating, it should be taken outside to an area that is designated as a toilet area. If the pup has a drink of water, take it outside. After a hearty play time, get the puppy outside. Before retiring for the night, get the dog out one last time. It is important that you go out with the dog. If the dog is simply

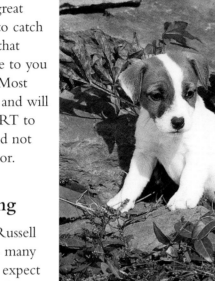

Start training your dog when it is a puppy. Reinforce the behavior you want with lots of praise or a treat. (photo by Jeannie Harrison/Close Encounters of the Furry Kind)

turned out in an enclosed area and the event happens, it is simply luck. You need to be with the dog and praise profusely when it eliminates where you want. Using the same area creates a scent that is user-friendly to the dog. You may feel silly, but it is a shorter route to success to teach the dog it is good to soil outdoors than to correct it for making a mistake indoors. To help prevent accidents, watch for any signals that indicate the dog is looking to relieve itself, such as sniffing or circling. Confining the student puppy when inside makes clean-up easier.

People that work full-time away from home have the most difficult time housetraining a puppy. It is asking too much to crate a puppy for long hours while at work. I suggest closing off the kitchen with doors or baby gates. Because the terrier is a smart little dog, it will find a distant room in a house to turn into a privy if the door is

For housetraining success, take your puppy outside when you get up, after it eats, after a play period, before bed and a few times in between.

carelessly left open. This is a favorite act in cold or rainy weather. Some Jack Russells find negative attention as charming to them as praise and take on a devil-may-care attitude toward housetraining.

Crate Training

If all else fails when housetraining a dog, a crate must be employed. Teaching the dog a command for elimination is recommended. The dog can sleep near your bedside in the crate. In the morning, attend to the dog first. Get it out quickly and praise it for appropriately relieving itself.

Crates are a dog owner's most useful tool. The crate is never a jail or punishment; rather, it is a den and safety zone for the dog. Buy a crate that's big enough for the full-grown dog to stand up and turn around in comfortably. To get your puppy used to the crate, at first feed it in there with the door open. Put a comfortable bed in the crate. Chew-resistant crate cushions that withstand soiling and sharp terrier teeth are useful. It is best if the crate is set up where the dog can watch the action of the household. It should be kept where there are no drafts or intense heat.

Never force the dog in the crate when teaching it to accept the confinement. Start by closing the crate door for a brief span of time. Release the dog only when it is settled. Soon the dog will pop in the crate on command without any fuss or resistance. Keep special toys that are just for crate time. Jack Russells love chew hooves and long strips of rolled rawhide. Never give them the kind with knots on the end, however, because they can choke on the knots. Pick up the crate toys and chews when the dog is not in the crate so they remain special for confinement time.

On occasion, an anxious owner will look for a dog from room to room only to find it sound asleep in its own crate with the door wide open. Jack Russells love their crate dens. Put one by a door and watch who hops right in, hoping it will be included on a trip. A well-behaved, crate-trained terrier is welcome most anywhere.

If you have a busy household, there are times when the dog is best put in its crate. If you are having a party where the doors will be opened many times, you can confine the dog to its crate to avoid an unwanted escape. A terrier will not tolerate too much frenzy among small children, and a crate can solve the problem.

TERRIER TROUBLES

I received a call one night from a woman in tears. She called to say the Jack Russell Terrier that her brother had given her would not let her or the children out of the kitchen. They were being held hostage by a dog on the other side of the door! I told her to call her brother, who lived nearby, to come remove the dog. This is a classic case of a dog with too much time on its paws and too little appropriate leadership from its family.

Lots of hardy exercise will help keep behavior problems to a minimum. A JRT that gets a chance to run and explore will have less desire (and less energy) to chew up your home.

The number-one cause of behavior problems in a JRT is lack of exercise. I cannot overstress how hard it is to tire out a Jack Russell Terrier. The rewards of living with a dog whose need for daily exercise are met are well worth the investment. Each day the dog must have meaningful exercise. It is also good for the owner to get out and get moving. A walk around the block is not enough. Get out and make it a walk around a big field. Most minor difficulties with a Jack Russell Terrier dim or disappear with sufficient exercise. The active time taken to fill the needs of the dog are well spent. This must be a daily commitment.

We had an exhausting dig one day when one of our dogs found a hole under a stump of a tree in the woods. I was hiking with the dogs, and Bolt 'Em Kodi found something to catch her interest. I came home to get tools to dig her out, feeling rather annoyed at her unauthorized hunting. It was not a simple dig. I returned to the house to get more tools and help. With two hours more of digging and using a chain saw, we dislodged the little dog. We never did find what she was fixed on inside the tree. Back at the house I took a snapshot of the spent workers. In the photo, the only fresh face was that of the little dog that had dug and bayed for two hours. She would have gone right back and repeated the entire process if she could have. It is very, very hard to tire a JRT. Their minds and bodies have a real need to be active.

In addition to a lot of physical action, a JRT thrives on a busy social life. Make sure a young dog is introduced to lots of social situations. It is good for puppies to meet and be handled by many different people. This helps to accustom the dog to strangers and will pay off when you take your pup to the veterinarian. When you go to the park or out for a walk, take the pup or young dog along with you and encourage people to interact with it. It is very important to develop social skills early on.

By acquainting your young JRT with as many people as possible, you will teach it to accept strangers. You want your dog to be friendly, not aggressive or shy.

Separation anxiety is a problem that arises with dogs. Never make a big fuss about leaving or returning home, and your dog will adopt your attitude that these are not significant events. Preventing separation anxiety is much better than trying to cure it. It is suggested that the dog learn to be ignored from time to time. JRTs like the center stagelight, so ignoring them is a discipline. Teach the dog to chill out cheerfully. Avoid conversation directed to the dog. Greet the dog last when you arrive home, and keep the greeting low-key. Later, plan a hearty exercise session as part of the daily routine.

I fell into a pattern that grew stressful in my own home. The minute I arrived home the dogs would all greet me with a full, excited, deafening cry and a profusion of springing energy. If the phone rang, nobody could hear it. I realized that I was encouraging this behavior by coming through the door and immediately taking them for their evening romp to the fields. The routine had to be changed. It is a lovely compliment to be greeted by a pack of happy dogs, but it's bad when things get out of control.

Managing Possessiveness

If a JRT gets possessive of toys or objects, simply remove them and do not allow such behavior. This is more of a problem in multiple-dog households. Never allow young children to take away anything a JRT is acting possessive over; it may take a family member of more authority than the youngest child to deal with such a situation smoothly. Any behavior of a young dog that is not favorable becomes a lot less "cute" as the dog matures. By actively encouraging the type of behavior that you want, from the moment you bring your dog home, you are working to ensure a happy relationship with it.

Inviting a Jack Russell Terrier into your life is truly adding a family member. You must be up to the rigors of accepting the dog's demand to be close to you in mind and body. If you understand you have a new shadow that is a touch naughty, you are set. Terrier troubles can result from simply misunderstanding the very real demands of this dog to be your companion. You will always need to be the leader of the dog and use a system of positive reinforcement to successfully keep the Jack Russell Terrier on an even keel.

Managing Mouthing

Mouthing problems take many forms. We expect pups to mouth and bite during teething from 3 to 6 months of age. But, be warned: Some pre- and post-teething pups mouth as obsessively as their 3- to -6-month-old counterparts. Natural though it may be, you must stop mouthing of flesh and valuables regardless of when it occurs, so that it does not become habitual.

Remember that you must establish that you are the leader of the house. If your Jack Russell displays possessiveness of an object, discourage it immediately. Cute puppy antics are no longer cute when the dog is an adult. (photo by Jeannie Harrison/Close Encounters of the Furry Kind)

Here are some tips:

1. Give your puppy wash rags that have been wetted, twisted out of excess water and frozen. Chewing on these relieves the discomfort of teething. Replace with a fresh one when it begins to thaw.

2. Give your puppy plenty of exercise and elicit play with proper toys.

General Problem-Solving Options

1. Don't let problems occur. Instead:

    a. keep your JRT confined when you can't prevent misbehavior,

    b. put out of reach anything that is or may be tempting, such as paper, garbage, personal belongings and paraphernalia such as remote controls,

c. close off areas with problem-making potential; shut the kids' bedroom door so your dog can't confiscate their toys, or block off the living room so it can't see or hear the paper boy's approach.

2. Divert your dog's attention from bad behavior by distracting it or rechanneling its energy:

a. To curtail attempts to chew woodwork or to dig in the garden, encourage it to play with a toy,

b. offer food while acclimating a sensitive or ticklish dog to having its feet massaged,

c. give obedience commands in rapid-fire succession to stop barking, jumping up or nipping.

CHAPTER 12

What You Should Know About Breeding

PEDIGREES AND QUALITIES

It is best to know as much as possible about the two dogs that are being considered for breeding. Study the pedigrees of both animals. It is a good practice to make a diagram of the pedigree before the mating. Blank forms may be obtained for doing this, and I advise using pencil while filling them out as it is easy to make errors following the diagram. Notes on coats, size and coloring are valuable. Any dog that has a JRTCA registration number should have the number kept on the pedigree. If the dog has earned a working certificate, it should be noted. The best matings are between known workers. If one is not a proven worker, better to breed it to a dog that is. The JRTCA has stored thousands of accurate pedigrees in its computer database for accuracy in the record keeping of its registry.

Look closely at the qualities of both animals in question. Does the stud dog's qualities complement any qualities of the bitch? You certainly should not breed dogs with known defects or serious faults. To create pups that are correct and can pass the required level of excellence to be registered is a worthy goal.

Your objective is to create a Jack Russell Terrier that will retain the ability to work and have a good temperament.

When you plot your pedigrees, look for common ancestors between the dog and bitch. If they have them, you will be inbreeding the line. Inbreeding is best left to experts. The JRTCA rules on inbreeding have been created to try to limit the pitfalls of the practice in protection of the breed. Inbreeding tends to manifest the best and the worst, often in the same litter. Outcrossing allows great diversity in the gene pool, even though the results are less predictable.

From time to time the results of a breeding will be truly exceptional. A "nick" occurs when the offspring are superior to the parents. Some breeders have such luck of the draw. Breeding is best left to those who study it seriously and work hard to produce dogs that will have a lasting good effect on the gene pool. I highly suggest any beginner leave the breeding to the experts.

Learning to breed healthy, hardy dogs takes time and experience. Creating a litter of puppies is truly best left to experts.

Reliable, reputable breeders are better qualified and experienced at producing quality puppies. Informed and talented breeders of Jack Russell Terriers can be found, and beginners can save themselves a lot of trial and error.

THE STUD DOG

A single stud dog can have a great influence on a breed. He may sire many bitches and leave his mark for generations to come. Consequently, the stud should be a fine example of a dog. He should be JRTCA registered and a known, successful earth worker.

If it is at all possible, the owner of the bitch should see and handle the dog to better know him. Is he correct and does he possess a good temperament? Even the best hunting dog should work as a team with the handler. Stud dogs should be friendly towards people.

The stud dog should be in good condition and fit. He should be well-muscled and well-nourished. He requires exercise and activity to be fit for breeding. Most breeders are honest about the qualities of their stud dog. Feel free to ask questions about the dog. Has he produced offspring that work below ground? How have his pups performed at working? Has he been tested for brucellosis? Has his hearing been tested to make sure that he is not deaf, even in one ear? Have his eyes been tested?

Do not breed to a stud dog with any known defects. Hearing and eye problems can be passed on to puppies by either parent or can reappear from a dog's ancestors. Testing prior to any

A quality stud dog will be in excellent condition and have an even temperament.

breeding helps prevent problems being perpetuated. Reputable breeders want to make sure they are not harming the breed by knowingly breeding any known defects.

THE BROOD BITCH

In order to have a healthy litter of puppies, it is important to have a healthy bitch that is up to the rigorous job of motherhood. She may have her first season sometime between the sixth and eighth month of her first year. She herself is not developed fully and needs to mature both mentally and physically before she is bred. She should be registered with the JRTCA prior to breeding. By the second heat cycle or later, she is better suited for the job. The bitch needs to be very healthy and in good condition. She should be taken to your veterinarian for a complete physical checkup. She can be given a serum agglutination test prior to breeding to make certain she is free of brucellosis. The results of the test can take a few days, so be sure to plan ahead.

The stud dog should be selected to enhance the qualities of the female and all arrangements should be made with its owner. The stud fee is sent with the bitch. If the stud owner agrees to take the pick of the litter, the agreement must be made in writing prior to the breeding.

The bitch should be watched carefully for indications of her season. There is a primary swelling of the vulva, which persists for four to five days. The discharge will be pale in color at first, then dark red. Some bitches do not show much discharge but will flag when receptive.

THE MATING

Traditionally the bitch is driven or sent by air to the residence of the stud dog to be bred. Individual bitches vary in their cycles, so it is wise to get the bitch to the stud six to nine days before any discharge is detected. Mating can be accomplished at some point after the tenth day in the cycle and usually must be completed before the seventeenth day. After this point in the cycle, the bitch will refuse the stud and may snap at his approaches. Often the couple will play and cavort when turned out together in the correct range of the accepting time of the cycle. The bitch will present herself to the stud and "flag," holding her tail to one side.

In a typical breeding schedule, the bitch will be bred on the tenth, twelfth, and fourteenth day of the cycle. Breeding the pair every forty-eight hours is advised.

A healthy litter of puppies can be produced only by a bitch that is mentally and physically mature.

Every effort should be made to assist the pair. Adjustments may be required for differences in heights. Holding the bitch may assist the stud. She may show fear if it is her maiden breeding and exhibit some hostility toward the stud. If you are not familiar with the bitch, prevent her from snapping. A muzzle is suggested to restrain her. Prevent sudden pulling away, sitting down or jumping.

If the mating is successful and the pair "tie," the hind leg of the stud can be gently lifted so they can stand facing away from each other. Again, it is important to prevent any pulling at this time. Any struggles to pull away may cause the stud dog injury. It may take up to a half hour or longer until the swelling of the male goes down and he can withdraw from the bitch.

It is wise to breed experienced stock. The difficulty increases if both are maidens. If the fifteenth day passes without a tie, have a veterinarian examine the pair. Immaturity, obstruction, or physiological reasons may be the problem. Some dogs are shy breeders and will not mate when observed by their masters. Some dogs will take a liking or disliking to the intended. Some bitches are polygamous, and some tend to want to mate with one dog and not another. Again, it is vital that the bitch be bred with only one stud during the heat.

Pregnancy Concerns

The diet of the pregnant bitch is very important. She needs to be maintained with a diet that is well-balanced while she is carrying and nursing her puppies. She will need all the necessary vitamins and minerals for the demand on her own body and the developing pups she carries. She should be kept fit during her pregnancy with suitable exercise.

The normal gestation period is between fifty-seven and sixty-three days. Most litters are delivered on the sixtieth to sixty-first day, but there are individual variations. Of course, the female should be checked during her pregnancy by the veterinarian. Though most deliveries present no medical problems, there is always the risk of complications that will require immediate veterinary attention. Be sure to seek medical help promptly if there are any problems in the whelping process.

WHELPING

The decision to breed brings one to the task of waiting for the arrival of the puppies. It may be necessary to assist the bitch during the whelping process. Be certain you can contact your veterinarian in case of complications and be able to get the bitch to the office promptly if required. Most Jack Russell Terriers are excellent mothers and often whelp without difficulty. There is always the chance, however, that a Caesarean section may be required if the labor is not productive. It is wiser to seek the help of your veterinarian early if a problem is detected than to wait until it becomes serious and the bitch is exhausted. Do not hesitate to consult with an expert to avoid problems.

An average Jack Russell pregnancy lasts about sixty days.

panel that drops or can be removed so the pups can crawl out and back in to rest when they develop.

Before going into labor, the bitch may refuse food. It is not unusual for a bitch in labor to vomit. The water bag around the puppy may been seen bulging out of the bitch's vulva. It lubricates the passage and may burst, indicating a puppy should be delivered in a few minutes. Do not interfere with the bitch if she is having a normal delivery. She will clean herself and the puppy and will often consume the placenta. Some breeders restrict the bitch from eating the placenta; I do not. If she shreds the umbilical cord too close to the pup's navel, it may continue to bleed. As a rule, I pinch off the cord and tie it with dental floss dipped in iodine before cutting it with scissors.

Prepare a suitable whelping area for the bitch away from household traffic and drafts. A whelping box should be a wooden box large enough to accommodate the dam and a number of puppies. Make it comfortable by lining the bottom with an old blanket. Make sure there is plenty of cushioning. A whelping box can be constructed with a

Be prepared to cut and tie the umbilical cord if necessary. Have all the supplies at hand when the bitch is near whelping so you won't be looking for everything you need at the last minute. Sterilize your scissors and use sterile gloves.

A wooden whelping box with plenty of cushioning will be appreciated by the dam and pups.

After whelping, the bitch may not want to leave her whelp to relieve herself. At this point I will close the door, make sure the pups are warm and carry her outside so that she may relieve herself while I stay with her. It will be a day or so before she cheerfully leaves her whelp to take care of her own needs. I keep food and fresh water near the whelping box so she may drink and eat as she desires.

The bitch should be able to easily get into the box and the puppies to stay in it securely. Keep visitors away from newborn puppies; the puppies do not need to be exposed to disease. Always keep the whelping box clean. Newspapers and soft cloth towels work well and can be changed easily. Newborn pups can propel themselves remarkably well and have a tendency to crawl under the bedding in the whelping box. For the first week, the pups should be

kept at a temperature of about 85 degrees F and draft free. Chilling is a danger to newborn pups.

Jack Russells love to try to have their babies in your bed or closet. If you show her the whelping box and it is available to her, your bitch can be directed to it easily. The best book to keep nearby and have studied well is the *Dog Owner's Home Veterinary Handbook* by Delbert G. Carlson, DVM, and James Giffin, MD (Howell Book House, 1992). It covers all aspects of canine obstetrics and postpartum information.

PUPPY PROCEDURES

Tail Docking

When the puppies are about three days old, their tails are shortened and the dewclaws are removed.

Newborn puppies should be kept warm and out of drafts. When not nursing, they spend a lot of time asleep.

The purpose of docking the tail is based on function and protection to the dog. There are times when the handler wants to reach in a hole and retrieve the dog. By being able to get hold of the dog's tail, one can gently draw the dog nearer, grasp the hind legs and extract the dog. The tail is meant to be a hand hold. Another reason for docking the tail is to prevent it from breaking while working below ground. While backing in tight earths, dogs with undocked tails have broken them, which disfigures the tail for the life of the dog.

There is no exact formula for tail docking, but here are suggestions. One wants the tail to be about four inches long on the adult dog. I recommend having a scant one-third of the tail removed. Oddly, the tails on the pups may vary. Thin tails have a tendency to be longer than thick tails. Some pick the point of the trim on the female just covering the vulva; on the male, the tail is cut at the point where the testes descend. Favoring a bit too much tail is less regrettable than taking off too much.

Experienced breeders help the veterinarian when the tails are docked so the exact length may be selected based on experience. Most veterinarians are happy to have your assistance and want the tails to be right.

Removing Dewclaws

The dewclaws are removed for efficient digging. If not removed, they may catch and tear, causing the dog great discomfort. Most Jack Russells have dewclaws on the front legs, but check to make sure there are none on the hind legs as well.

A pup's tail is docked so that as an adult, it can serve as a hand hold.

Keep Your Veterinarian Involved

Have your veterinarian check over the puppies. Worm them as he or she suggests, and arrange for the first inoculations to be given before the pups leave at eight weeks for their new homes.

Make sure the bitch is well attended after whelping. Watch for trouble, and alert your veterinarian if any problems arrive. Let the veterinarian examine her after the birth to make sure everything is normal and none of the birth matter has been retained. Make sure the dam's milk is flowing well and that none of her breasts get hard or hot to the touch. Mastitis (infection of the mammary glands) will require treatment suggested by your veterinarian. Any problem with a nursing dog requires immediate correction.

Eclampsia or "milk fever" is a problem seen in small dogs. It is caused by an upset in the calcium regulatory system that leads to a low calcium level in the blood. It is often seen in the first three weeks of lactation. The early symptoms may be very subtle. They may be noted as a mild tremor in the muscles. The bitch may become restless and pant or whine. She may walk stiffly or have a painful look to her face, almost like a grimace. If ignored, the bitch is in grave danger. Eclampsia causes the temperature of the dog to rise, which makes for more problems. If her temperature goes over 104 degrees, you must treat her as if for heat stroke. Get immediate veterinary help. Intravenous calcium solutions may give the bitch immediate relief. Only the veterinarian can regulate the correct amount to prevent cardiac arrhythmia. The veterinarian may prescribe supplements appropriate to prevent eclampsia. If a bitch has ever exhibited milk fever, it is likely that she will have the experience again.

ENSURING GOOD HOMES FOR THE PUPPIES

Selecting the right home for each puppy you sell is an enormous responsibility. Make it very clear to the buyer that you are there with an open and friendly mind to help him or her at any stage of the dog's life. Sometimes just a little help and some good suggestions can enable the owner and dog to work out any minor problems that may arise.

Think long and hard before you sell a puppy to a household where the people work long hours and are gone more than they are home. It may well be that these owners will find it too difficult to give the dog the time and attention it needs to be a well-rounded pet. This dog will probably think of things to do that will not please its new family. Boredom makes for some very creative behavior that may horrify a homeowner.

No puppy should be sold to a household where there is no containment. The dog will quickly be killed by a car or wander off. No fencing other than a capped kennel can be trusted to hold a Jack Russell Terrier while the owner is away. The dog can climb and dig out of good situations in search of adventure if left unattended. Tying or chaining a Jack Russell Terrier is unthinkable. Trolley systems are not acceptable or safe.

It is inadvisable to sell a Jack Russell Terrier puppy to a household with many young children. In fact, I suggest that these puppies not live in households with children under six years old. They cannot take the high-pitched activity level that young children seem to radiate. Abuse will not be tolerated, even when it is unintentional.

Finally, for those cat lovers who want a small dog, I do not suggest the Jack Russell Terrier. Keep in mind that if no fox is available, a cat will do just fine. Birds and sometimes horses do not fare well with this terrier, either. Many JRTs can be trained to leave other pets alone, but if you are not present, you should not expect them to "remember" this training at all times. It is simply asking too much of a dog whose entire history has been as a hunting dog.

Some people need a little help with dog behavior questions. As the dog's breeder, by being open and helpful you may prevent the dog being sent to a shelter and its possible death from misunderstanding. It does a great deal of good to talk to the people who have your pups on a regular basis. If this is too big a task, perhaps you are breeding too many dogs. Make it very clear that if there is ever a serious problem, you wish to help. If this means taking the dog back on a temporary basis, do so. If the dog needs to be placed in a different home because of the circumstances of the family, then by all means help the owner place the dog. The JRTCA Russell Rescue is not a service to help free breeders of responsibility for their offspring. Helping the dog to have a good life is part of the responsibility of creating life.

The Jack Russell Terrier Club of America has published a list of questions for the potential buyer of puppies to ask breeders and vice versa. They are reprinted here with permission.

As a breeder, it is your responsibility to place the puppies in homes where they will be given the best care.

Instructions for Puppy Buyers

Ask the Breeder. . .

Are the sire and/or the dam on the premises? May I see them?
How many pups were in the litter?
Are the sire and dam JRTCA registered? If not, why not?
Do you offer a guarantee? (Ask to see the written guarantee.)
Is the pup guaranteed to be registerable?
How many years have you bred dogs?
How many litters do you breed a year?
May I see the pedigree?
Are there any known genetic problems in the dog's pedigree?
May I see the medical history of the pups? Is there a vet health certificate included with the pup?
Does the puppy come with a complete pedigree and Breeder's Certificate so I can register it in the future? Is it signed? Does the pedigree include four or more generations?

When you go to select a puppy, ask yourself if the pup appears to meet the Standard for the breed. More important, ask yourself if you will make a commitment to care for the needs of an active, attentive Jack Russell Terrier. (photo by Jeannie Harrison/Close Encounters of the Furry Kind)

Ask Yourself. . .

Do the parents have the kind of temperament and personality that I desire in my pup?
Are the premises clean?
Are the dogs happy?
Do they appear to be healthy?
Does this dog appear to meet the JRTCA's registry requirements?

Does this dog appear to meet the breed Standard?
Is the breeder breeding to the breed Standard?
Is the breeder putting any restrictions on the sale and if so, are they reasonable?
Is a Jack Russell really the right dog for me? Can I cope with its level of activity?

Instructions for Breeders

Ask the Buyer. . .

Do you have proper facilities to care for this dog?
Do you have a fenced area?
Will the dog be supervised for its own safety?
Do you realize that owning a dog is an expense?
Do you realize that owning a dog is an everyday thing and a serious commitment for many years to come, not a fad of the moment?
Have you owned, or do you own, other dog(s)?
What happened to them?
Will you keep in touch as to progress?
Do you plan to breed? Show? Work?
Will you call me first if you ever feel you have to place the dog in another home?

Ask Yourself. . .

Does the buyer appear to want a dog for the right reason?
Do your dogs like this person?
Is the buyer gentle with the dog?
Is the buyer confident with the dog?
Are all family members in agreement with this purchase?

If selling a pup, make sure that the new owner will provide a suitable environment for it.

Does the buyer have the time to see that the Jack Russell gets the large amount of exercise that he requires?

How many hours in the day is the buyer actually at home?

Most importantly, does the buyer fully understand what is involved in owning a Jack Russell Terrier?

When one creates life, one becomes responsible for it as long as that life lasts. If this isn't something you can manage, then you should not breed puppies at all. With each puppy sold at eight weeks of age you should provide documentation for the new owner that includes your name, address and telephone number. Keep the buyer's address and phone number yourself, and check on the dog from time to time. If for any reason the relationship does not work out, make sure it is clear that you will do what you can to satisfy the person that has purchased your puppy. It is wise to have a contract that clearly delineates responsibilities. If you have carefully asked all the right questions and found the family suitable, it is less likely the puppy will be returned.

Going beyond your own evaluation, make sure the puppy likes the people it is leaving with—you should be able to tell. If you do not feel comfortable with the people in question, do not sell the dog to them. By preventing a mismatch, you will save a lot of grief all around. Your puppy cannot speak for itself. You must have a decided hand in its fate.

Breeding dogs is rarely a money-making undertaking. As a breeder, you may want to keep a puppy from the resulting litter, hoping for a good dog. The litter was not created for money. It is more important to provide the dog you have created with a good life than to ever think you will gain financially from breeding dogs. Encourage each person that buys a dog from you to become a member of the Jack Russell Terrier Club of America. The club is an educational organization whose publications and services are invaluable to the Jack Russell fancier.

For those people that buy a dog from you, encourage spaying or neutering if they want to keep the dog as a pet. You may have created a fine example of the breed and hope others will know of its merits, but most puppies go to pet homes. You might want to offer a refund of some of the cost of a puppy if the buyer spays or neuters the dog. Not only is the Jack Russell Terrier not for everybody, breeding them certainly isn't, either!

From time to time a defect may appear in a puppy. If at one year the puppy cannot be registered with the Jack Russell Terrier Club of America, let the breeder know. On occasion, the veterinarian will find a problem that makes registering the dog impossible. Inform the breeder if this occurs. It may be that the dog has a testicle that does not descend, that a bad bite is present or that the dog suffers from luxating patella (slipped knee). The breeder will want to have this information to prevent repeating the mating. A defect may show up that has not manifested in the pedigree to the breeder's best knowledge. If it does, a good breeder will want to know immediately. The JRTCA keeps records of any defects to help expand knowledge and protect the breed through better understanding and genetic study.

Reputable breeders want to breed the best dogs they humanly can bring forth by selection based on careful study. Keep in mind that an open and friendly relationship is the desired goal of any good breeder. A good breeder will want you to be happy and wants what is best for the future generations of the dog.

CHAPTER 13

Special Care for the Older Dog

J ack Russell Terriers seem to act like puppies even into their senior years. However, they may sleep more than they used to, or seem a little more laid back. Some become set in their ways and routines. Certain older dogs have less patience with boisterous children than when they were young. Often, however, the only hint of senior years is a bit of gray on the face. The senior dog may have a few missing teeth from breaking roots away from earthen tunnels, or it may have diminished hearing and eyesight.

MONITOR YOUR SENIOR'S HEALTH

It is very important to keep the senior dog in good health. It should have a yearly veterinary examination to maintain its care. Its teeth should be checked and cleaned if necessary. Sometimes broken teeth need to be removed.

The senior dog should not be allowed to become overweight. Many older dogs keep a high energy level if around other dogs. However, if it is the only dog in the household, a senior may be inclined to be less active. Adjust the dog's food intake to keep it trim. Feeding table scraps is not recommended. The senior dog may be good at asking for snacks, but resist its pleas, as it is not good for the dog to carry

As your terrier ages, it may become more sedentary.

extra pounds. It may be helpful to wet the senior dog's food to soften the kibble.

EUTHANASIA

If your older dog is in pain and the quality of its life is lessening, it may be time to make a decision with the veterinarian to release the dog from serious suffering. The doctor may consult with you on the difficult decision to put a beloved dog to sleep. It is possible to hold and comfort the dog while the injection is given that painlessly and quickly ends life.

Saying good-bye to a dog is often one of the most difficult things we face as dog lovers. A great deal of thought must go into the decision to end a friend's life, even by this humane method. The quality of your dog's life must be taken into consideration. It is not kind to allow a dog to endure constant pain or suffering.

Your veterinarian will be honest and direct in helping you manage a dog that is declining. There may be medications or treatments that can prolong or improve the life of a fading friend, and so it may be possible to gain a little more time with the help of the veterinarian's guidance.

If the decision is made to euthanize the dog, expect sorrow. Allow yourself and your family to feel the grief that follows this process. It is never easy to say good-bye to a dog that has been loved. To any dog that has brought a great deal of

Although a senior terrier slows down, it still needs to be exercised. Don't stop taking your dog to activities.

Your JR's inner beauty lasts forever.

Dogs that have been with us for awhile provide so much comfort.

closeness and companionship, saying good-bye is heart-wrenching.

At first, nothing can soothe the loss. The dog is watched for. A sudden shadow out of the corner of the eye becomes the dog. Memories are uncovered. The empty dog bed gets put tearfully aside. The leash by the door or favorite toy triggers tears again. Remaining hairs on clothing or furniture get a loving pat or are saved to soothe the hurting heart. The memories burn strongly as we sit by the fire and recall the good times. The emotions felt are both intense and painful. Time heals too slowly, if at all.

Confiding in an understanding friend can be of some help. There are also books written on the subject of pet loss that can assist you in understanding and accepting the emotions surrounding your loss. Some veterinary colleges, such as the College of Veterinary Medicine at the University of California, Davis, and Cornell University's Veterinary College, offer pet loss support hotlines staffed by veterinary student volunteers who are trained by a professional grief counselor. Literature relating to pet loss and grief is maintained by the hotline and available to callers who request information. The number for the Cornell hotline is 607-253-3932. Phone hours are Tuesday, Wednesday and Thursday from 6:00 to 9:00 P.M. EST. You can also write or make contributions by contacting the Pet Loss Support Hotline/Companion Animal Hospital, Box 35, College of Veterinary Medicine, Cornell University, Ithaca, New York 14853-6401. Cornell has a Web site at http://www.vet.cornell.edu/public/petloss/. The University of California, Davis, School of Veterinary Medicine is staffed by students. The number is 916-752-4200. The service is free (except for the cost of phone calls) and is available Monday through Friday, 6:30 to 10:30 P.M. PST.

My friend Joan LaPlace sent me these words when I lost my dear dog Nester. They remain a comfort.

Old Dogs Do Not Die

We have a secret you and I
That no one else shall know
For who but I can see you lie,
Each night, in fireglow?
And who but I can reach my hand
before I go to bed,
and feel the living warmth of you
and touch your silken head?
And only I walk woodland paths,
and see ahead of me,
your small form racing with the wind
so young again and free.
And only I can see you swim
in every brook I pass...
And, when I call, no one but I can see the bending
grass...

—*Unknown*

You never lose your memories of your pet.

CHAPTER 14

The Breed Club of America

The Jack Russell Terrier Club of America (JRTCA) was founded in 1976 by Ailsa Crawford of Far Hills, New Jersey. The JRTCA was incorporated as a nonprofit organization in January of 1987. In October 1987, Mrs. Crawford resigned as president. She was awarded a lifetime membership and a position on the board of directors as president emeritus in honor of her eleven years as president and founder of the Jack Russell Terrier Club of America and Registrar. She remains devoted to the Jack Russell, and she and her husband, Harden Crawford II, advise the club. She continued to operate and manage the club office and registry until 1994.

The JRTCA office is now located in Lutherville, Maryland. The club sponsors a National Trial that attracts approximately 1,000 Jack Russells (and their owners) each October. It is the largest show in the world devoted exclusively to Jack Russell Terriers. The JRTCA offers many member services and publications. It is managed by a board of directors and several committees that direct the varied aspects of running the club at a national level. The club magazine, *True Grit*, is printed bimonthly. It includes educational information concerning all aspects of the Jack Russell Terrier. The JRTCA is the largest breed club for the Jack Russell in the world.

The JRTCA sponsors terrier events where members share their stories and have fun.

THE BREED REGISTRY

The Jack Russell Terrier Club of America's breed registry has been specifically designed to maintain the Jack Russell Terrier as a healthy working breed, free from genetic faults and characteristics that would be detrimental to the breed. While other registries allow registration of entire litters at birth, the JRTCA registry requires that each dog be registered at one year of age and not before, and that each be evaluated on the individual terrier's own merits. The registry maintains detailed records of each dog registered. Having registered parents does not automatically guarantee that a terrier can be registered. Each application for registration must be accompanied by these required documents:

• A veterinary certificate designed specifically for the Jack Russell. It must be completed and signed by a licensed veterinarian. Completion includes examination for genetic defects that have been known to appear in the breed. A terrier must pass this examination to be registered.

• A pedigree of at least four complete generations, signed by the breeder (more than four generations is encouraged). The JRTCA will not accept any terrier that is inbred according to the club's inbreeding policy. No father-to-daughter, mother-to-son or brother-to-sister matings are allowed. Half-brother-to-half-sister matings are permitted only once within three generations if there is an ancestor that is common to both the sire and dam. More than one half-sister-to-half-brother mating is allowed unless one or more ancestors exist on both the sire's and the dam's sides of the pedigree. A generation is defined as the complete lineage of both the sire and the dam. If a pedigree does not meet these criteria, an exception will be recognized only if the inbreeding coefficient is computed at 15 percent or less. The JRTCA has implemented a computerized pedigree database to maintain and verify accurate pedigree information.

• A stud service certificate signed by the owner of the sire, verifying that the stud dog was bred to the dam of the terrier applying for registration. Color photographs of the dog standing on a firm surface, showing each side and the front of the terrier, are required in order to evaluate the terrier's general adherence to the breed Standard. The veterinarian is required to sign the photographs of the dog, thereby verifying that this is the dog he or she has examined for registration.

The owner of a terrier applying for registration must be a current member of the JRTCA. Terriers are turned down for registration for not meeting the breed Standard or for any genetic fault. Those dogs that fail to meet the qualifications for the breed registry are also recorded by the JRTCA, and these records are retained in the club office. Terriers that are issued a certificate of recording qualify to compete for JRTCA Trial and Natural Hunting Certificates. Any terrier possessing a genetic fault will not be accepted for recording unless it is spayed or neutered.

A dog must be at least one year old before it can be registered with the club.

For registration purposes, the club will ask for color photographs of the dog, showing each side and the front.

CHAPTER 15

Headliners

I have made a serious study of Jack Russell Terriers in my years of involvement with the breed, working them in the field as many others do. It gives me great satisfaction to serve as a working judge for the JRTCA and to get to see the success of the breed's work in the field. I have the privilege of serving the JRTCA as a conformation judge. It is an honor to get to view and handle many quality dogs and bitches in the United States. Some of the finest Jack Russell Terriers living today have been bred in the United States. Working and making a study of dogs is an ongoing life process. I am but one voice in praise of excellence.

I would like to showcase some outstanding terriers. This is just a sampling of some remarkable dogs that are both conformationally sound and excellent hunting dogs. They have all produced offspring that also hunt. These animals carry the torch of what is desirable and well-rounded. In my opinion, the mind of the animal in the field cannot be viewed when led around a show ring. All these featured dogs have been successful showing and working.

A dog that is "fine-looking" clearly is not enough for those who truly love the breed as a "working" or "workable" terrier. The "bathing suit" competition of the conformation ring does not represent the JRT's talent. It is in the field that the true grit of the dog is tested.

I am sure many will agree with me that the animals featured in this chapter are fine examples of the breed. Three of the dogs have been featured in the Stud Book, Volume IV, printed by the Jack Russell Terrier Club of America. Some were voted by the Breeder's Committee for inclusion because of their early influence upon the terrier in the United States. I have included some of these dogs' offspring, who carry on the working tradition and the conformation best fit for earthwork.

When pondering what dogs would be good examples to include in this segment of the text, I found many were closely related. The dogs are presented in alphabetical order. None of these dogs was chosen to promote it to the exclusion of others. I picked working terriers that have held up over the test of time. Without contest, this is the most simple unifying truth about them. There has been time to see what their descendants have done and produced. It surprised me to find so many of them interconnected. A good dog is a good dog.

Camelot Derby.

All the dogs included have chests that allow them to travel deeply into the earth. Look at how they appear keen and ready. They are well-muscled and fit animals, with good fronts and powerful hindquarters. Although this is just a tiny selection of some fine terriers, there are many in the United States. This simply points out a few fine dogs of the right stuff who will endure. Many are now older, but still are flexible and vigorous, a credit to their tradition and history of work.

CAMELOT DERBY

Derby was bred by Linda Toscano in the United States and is a son of Flare. He is owned by Michael Bailiff and Terry Clower. Derby has earned the JRTCA

All of the dogs featured in this chapter are well-built for work. Shown above: White Gate Bomber.

Fox Run Risk.

worked with a recognized pack of foxhounds in America until the practice was prohibited by the Masters of Foxhounds Association.

Risk has placed highly in many competitions over the years. She has been at the top of many of the JRTCA National Trials as Best and Best Working Terrier. Her record is remarkable for producing winning terriers in competition. Her offspring are excellent workers. Linda points out that "Risk's descendants continue to improve and greatly influence the Jack Russell today. She has produced many outstanding offspring." Her name appears in the pedigrees of many of the fine working terriers of the United States today. Her good

Bronze Medallion for Special Merit in the Field for working red fox, groundhog and opossum. He has won at the National Jack Russell Trial back to back and has sired winners of National Trials. He is a handsome dog with a ready-for-work look.

Derby is described as having a "happy-go-lucky attitude." When out with other dogs he is "the boss," but his owners report that he is as affectionate as a puppy. Derby has made a mark on the breed and is found in many pedigrees.

FOX RUN RISK

Risk was bred in the United States by Sandra Ferber and belongs to Linda Cowasjee. Her sire is Riverview Flare. She earned the JRTCA Bronze Medallion for hunting red fox, raccoon and groundhog. She is one of the few terriers that

Foxfield Garth.

Foxwarren Floyd.

Maven's Tailor.

looks and inclination to enjoy work have definitely been passed along.

FOXFIELD GARTH

Garth was bred by Marcy Cross in the United States and is owned by Debbie and Paul McWilliams. He is a keen working dog and earned the JRTCA Bronze Medallion. He has sired many winning dogs and bitches in the field and ring. Garth has won at the JRTCA National Trial and many other trials. He is a dog with a lot of personality and is very affectionate with children. Garth is a son of Flare, who carries the blood of Foxwarren Floyd. He enjoys working and has what best can be described as a humorous and lovable personality.

FOXWARREN FLOYD

Floyd was bred by Eddie Chapman of Great Britain and brought to the United States by Dr. John and Barbara Lowery. He had an outstanding winning career in the ring and at work. His name appears in the pedigrees of many of the other dogs listed in this chapter. Floyd had a great impact on improving American Jack Russell Terriers. He was put to many bitches and made his mark both in conformation and hunting ability. Although now his name is way back in pedigrees, his good looks appear strongly from the past. Floyd had a wonderful disposition, and many of the terriers that love small children carry his blood.

Floyd had a long life in the United States and was a beloved companion and stud dog that loved to work in the field. Many seasoned Jack Russell enthusiasts can remember his outstanding presence. He was such a fine-looking dog that your eye would go right to him in admiration. Floyd will long be remembered. He was a remarkable dog, a monumental example of a Jack Russell Terrier. His descendants have been fine working dogs and bitches.

MAVEN'S TAILOR

Tailor was bred by Alf Edmonds of Great Britain and is owned by Jack and Terri Batzer in the United States. He earned the JRTCA Bronze Medallion. Tailor has great presence and wonderful structure. He is put together well from head to toe—even the bones of this dog are handsome! Tailor's name appears in many of the best working terriers' pedigrees of today. He is a top winning dog and continues in his senior years to win against younger dogs at JRTCA National Trials and many competitions.

One of the finest traits of Tailor is his small chest, which compresses easily to the touch. Many older dogs become rigid, but not Tailor. As a veteran, he still feels like a puppy. This flexibility makes it easy for a dog to follow a fox deep in the ground in hopes of bolting it. It is something both necessary and desired of the working terrier used as a stud dog. Tailor has a good smooth coat and is overall one fine dog. He passes his traits on through his descendants. Not many dogs are in such remarkable shape into their senior years.

Tailor has been known to get out and go hunting any chance he gets—even to this day. His instinct to hunt is deeply ingrained. He is a great dog that has certainly made his mark in American Jack Russell Terrier history.

NORTH COUNTRY PINOCCHIO

Pinney, as he is affectionately called by his owner and breeder, Norah Risley, is a Jack Russell for all seasons. His sire is Riverview Flare. Pinocchio did well in the show ring for a number of years. He is known as an excellent hunting dog, earning his Bronze Medallion for hunting red fox, raccoon, and groundhog.

Pinocchio is a handsome animal, a good hunter and an excellent competitive agility dog. He is a very versatile dog. His owner says with

North Country Pinocchio.

Riverview Flare.

WHITE GATE BOMBER

Bomber, owned and bred by William and Nancy Breakstone of the United States, is an excellent hunting dog. His sire is the aforementioned Flare. He has earned his JRTCA Bronze Medallion for locating and working red fox, raccoon, groundhog and opossum. He has been placed Best or Reserve over twenty times and has thrice been Reserve Best at the JRTCA National Trial.

Bomber has a fine temperament as both a companion and a hunting dog. He moves without effort and has a nice, small chest. His coat is a traditional straight coat with an overcoat for protection and a good undercoat. In maturity he has remained flexible.

great wisdom, "There is no end to what these terriers can do with the proper training. They need and should have a job, and to that end, we must challenge them daily."

RIVERVIEW FLARE

Flare was bred by JoAnn Kleinman in the United States and owned by Sandra Ferber. This dog's name probably appears in more American pedigrees than nearly any other dog. Without a doubt, he has had an enormous impact on the gene pool of many American working terriers alive today. Flare won in the ring and earned his JRTCA Bronze Medallion for working red fox, raccoon and groundhog. Foxwarren Floyd is his grandsire. Flare is a well-balanced terrier and has exceptionally good looks. Many of his descendants carry his traits and desire to work below ground.

White Gate Bomber.

The Jack Russell Terrier Club of America's Breeder's Code of Ethics

The policies set forth herein outline the ethical breeding practices expected of all JRTCA members. Members registering a kennel prefix are required to acknowledge and agree to adhere to the Code of Ethics by signature to this document. JRTCA Breeders directory subscribers and Stud Book applicants are required to sign the Code of Ethics with each application. All those who are signatory to the Code may be subject to a kennel inspection (with notice) at any time deemed necessary by the JRTCA Board of Directors, and may be subject to penalties being levied should substantiated violations to the Code of Ethics be incurred.

LITTER PLANNING/BREEDING

(1) All breeding stock must be registered prior to use for breeding; both parents must be JRTCA registered prior to mating.

(2) Conscientiously plan each litter; carefully select stud dog and bitch to be mated based on pedigrees, the parent's conformation (according to the JRTCA breed standard), working ability, and temperament.

(3) Breed only adults which are free from inheritable defects, and avoid the introduction of any detrimental factors. Any new defects encountered should be reported to the JRTCA Breeders Committee before the mating in question.

(4) Adhere to the JRTCA's current policy on inbreeding. Note: When planning a breeding, any questions concerning the above should be referred to the Registrar (club office) or Chairman of the JRTCA Breeders Committee before the mating in question.

(5) Breed only healthy, mature bitches over one year of age, preferably not before the second heat, allowing sufficient spacing between litters. It is recommended that bitches over the age of eight (8) years not be bred without prior examination, consultation and approval by an attending veterinarian.

(6) Do not breed any bitch to more than one stud dog during a single heat period.

Should a second breeding occur unintentionally, the resulting litter must be sold as pets only with a spay/neuter agreement and no pedigree provided.

STUD SERVICES

(1) Register all stud dogs in the JRTCA registry prior to use for breeding.

(2) Breed stud dogs only to those outside adult bitches who appear registerable/recordable (i.e. generally meet the JRTCA breed standard, are free of genetic defects of any kind, have a minimum of two generations of pedigree, and are NOT owned by a member of a conflicting organization or registered with any all-breed kennel club or conflicting organization).

(3) Require a current (within six months) negative Brucella test on all bitches prior to mating, and be able to provide same for the stud dog to owner of the bitch.

(4) Provide a signed and dated JRTCA Stud Certificate. It is recommended that an original signed and dated stud certificate for each puppy in the litter be provided at the time of the whelping.

HEALTH & GENERAL CARE

(1) Keep all breeding stock under clean and sanitary conditions.

(2) Provide housing and run areas of adequate size with safety features specific to the character and exercise requirements of Jack Russell Terriers. Do not kennel Jack Russell Terriers on wire flooring.

(3) Provide maximum health protection through regular inoculations, worming, and periodic veterinarian exams. BAER and CERF Tests are recommended.

(4) A semi-annual brucella test is recommended for all breeding stock (dogs and bitches).

(5) Maintain mental health and well-being through human contact and exercise on a regular basis.

SALES

(1) Carefully screen all potential buyers, educating them on all the aspects of the Jack Russell Terrier.

(2) Sell only to proper homes; i.e. individuals who give adequate evidence they have a satisfactory environment, and will give the terrier the proper care, attention and exercise required for a Jack Russell Terrier.

(3) Accurately represent the qualities of your terriers to the purchaser.

Puppies should be at least eight weeks of age before they leave their dam and littermates.

Do not knowingly use misleading or untruthful statements in selling or advertising.

(4) Puppies must be at least eight (8) weeks of age prior to leaving the breeder's possession; this includes shipping, any other type of delivery, or buyer pick-up under any circumstances.

(5) Spay or neuter any mature dog/bitch with a known genetic defect or that is going to be retired prior to selling or placing for adoption.

(6) Place puppies possessing a genetic defect only with a written, signed and dated agreement requiring spay/neuter at the earliest possible date. Do not provide a pedigree until proof of spay/neuter is received.

(7) Provide buyers with health and general care information at the time of the sale, including but not limited to, feeding and general care instructions, a veterinarian health certificate, and a record of worming and inoculations. A several day supply of the puppy's current food is recommended.

(8) Provide buyers with the paperwork necessary for registration. Provide a complete pedigree showing a minimum of four generations (five generations preferred), showing height, coat, color and any other information known in lineage: pedigree also should include 1) name, description and birth date of the terrier, 2) name,

address and phone number of the breeder, and 3) signature of the breeder. Also provide a stud certificate completed and signed by the owner of the sire. As much information as possible should be included on the pedigree (i.e., heights, registration numbers, etc.).

(9) Provide buyers with a JRTCA Puppy Packet. (Note: Puppy packets are available free of charge by contacting the JRTCA office.)

(10) Be responsible for terriers sold for their lifetime. If a purchaser cannot keep a terrier you have sold, make every effort to assist them in finding an appropriate home. If the owners are unable to place a terrier for whatever reason, or a displaced terrier which you have bred is located in a shelter or through Russell Rescue, be prepared to take the terrier back and be responsible for placing it in an appropriate home.

(11) Do not knowingly sell or consign puppies or adults to pet shops, brokers, or puppy mills, nor supply terriers for raffles, prizes, or similar projects.

(12) Use sales contracts or written agreements to cover any special provision of sales or service transactions.

(13) Be aware of, and adhere to, the JRTCA's policy on co-ownerships and be sure that the proper contracts are in place accordingly.

(photo by Winter Churchill Photography)

Jack Russell Terrier Clubs of the World

There are Jack Russell Terrier Clubs around the world. A few have aligned themselves with kennel clubs in their respective countries. The clubs that are affiliated with the Jack Russell Terrier United World Federation are united in the preservation of the Jack Russell Terrier as a working terrier.

The Jack Russell Terrier Club of Great Britain was organized by Romaine Moore. There were founding members and committees. A number of regions send regular newsletters, and there is an annual magazine. Many terrier trials are held in Great Britain, and a National Trial is held in August.

The overseas affiliates of the Jack Russell Terrier Club of Great Britain are the United States, Canada, South Africa, Namibia, Japan, Germany, Australia, New Zealand and Sweden. Other affiliates are the JRTCs of Scotland and East Anglia. The overseas regions affiliated with the JRTCGB are Sweden, Finland and Zimbabwe. Great Britain, being the country of origin of the Jack Russell Terrier, has served as the parent club for the affiliated clubs of the world.

The Jack Russell Terrier is loved around the world. (photo by Jeannie Harrison/Close Encounters of the Furry Kind)

The Jack Russell Terrier Club of Canada was formed in 1989 by a group of Jack Russell owners at a trial during the lunch break. The structure of the JRTCC is similar to that of the JRTCA. Its formation committee met on September 17, 1989. The breed Standard of the JRTCGB was adopted, and the JRTCA system of registration was formed later.

The Jack Russell Terrier Club of Japan was formed in March 1996 by Ann N. Narori and Kirk and Kumiko Hubbard. They were all members of the JRTCA. A monthly newsletter is produced and there are quarterly gatherings. The club is planning to build a trial site outside Tokyo. It is the only established Jack Russell Club in Asia.

Finland has a club as a region of the JRTCGB in Suomi Finland. It was founded in April of 1995. The club holds conformation gatherings, trailing and locating, go-to-ground competitions and hunts.

Sweden's club is affiliated with the JRTCGB. It was formed in 1994. The club offers competitions.

The Jack Russell Club of Germany was formed in 1996.

Zimbabwe is a region of the JRTCGB founded by Sandhi Rogerson and David Doig in 1996. It mainly is a hunting organization.

The Jack Russell Club of Namibia was founded in 1994 by Sandhi Rogerson and Trix Farrelman. The club has regular trial and active hunting members. Their annual National Trial is in June of each year. The club adopted the JRTCA registration system. It is divided into four regions with committees and prints an annual magazine and regular newsletters. The club is affiliated with both the JRTCGB and the Jack Russell Terrier Club of South Africa.

The Jack Russell Terrier Club of South Africa was founded in January of 1981 by thirty members. Trials include conformation, go-to-ground and racing competitions. The club has quarterly magazines and six regions with full committees. The National Trial is in May. The trial system has three tiers. After one year of age, a terrier is inspected by an A-Judge for adherence to the breed Standard and issued a breeder's registration number. Pups of parents with a breeder's registration number get a listing number and certificate of origin or pedigree, issued by the Breed Records Office. Full registration is granted on gaining a Gameness or Working Certificate, both of which are earned in the field. The club is an active hunting club. It is affiliated with the JRTCGB.

The Jack Russell United World Federation (JRUWF) exists to unite all JRT Clubs of the

The Jack Russell United World Federation is devoted to preserving the working JRT.

world to form a strong network for the purpose of insuring the preservation of the *working* Jack Russell Terrier. It opposes affiliation with, or influence by, any organization or persons whose beliefs or actions might result in practices considered detrimental to the breed. It opposes recognition to the Jack Russell Terrier by any kennel club throughout the world. It serves to unify all JRT Clubs to the same basic breed Standard used internationally. The Federation promotes communication between all Jack Russell Terrier Clubs of the world and it opposes all anti-field sport movements, particularly those opposed to the preservation of fox hunting and terrier work. The Federation assists and encourages cooperative effort between Jack Russell Terrier Clubs of all nations, their members and breeders to achieve the foregoing objectives and purposes. The Federation is not operated for a profit.

Jack Russell Terrier Club of America—Affiliated Clubs

The following local clubs/networks are affiliated with the JRTCA; their purpose is to provide activities for, and communication between, JR enthusiasts within a local geographic area. They share the JRTCA's goals and objectives for the Jack Russell. Please contact these groups if you are interested in local terrier activities in your geographic area.

The Arkansas JRT Club
c/o Joanna Godwin
2008 King David Park Rd.
Little Rock, AR 72210
(501) 661-7339

The Bayou JRT Club
c/o Sean and Kathryn Quinlan
1008 Harmony St.
New Orleans, LA 70115
(617) 884-4338

Buckeye State JRT Club
c/o Judy Churchfield
1985 Hamburg Rd.
Lancaster, OH 43130
(740) 681-9640

Carolinas JRT Club
c/o Donna Hastings
317 Aderholdt Rd.
Bessemer City, NC 28016
(704) 435-5688

Dixie JRT Club
c/o Debbie Graydon
101 West Fleming Rd.
Montgomery, AL 36105
(205) 281-8085

Georgia JRT Club
c/o Debbie Johnson
2200 Cloud Land Dr.
Kennesaw, GA 30152
(770) 427-1618

Gold Coast Terrier Network
c/o Jack Fawkes
33333 Camerton Rd.
Zephyrhills, FL 33543
(813) 788-4266

The Gulf Coast JRT Club
c/o Tressie Cowen
RR 1, Box 156C
Burton, TX 77835
(409) 289-5034

The Intermountain JRT Club
c/o Tonya Adams
4675 West 11200 South
Payson, UT 84651
(801) 465-1461

JRT Network of Northern California
c/o Marjorie and Scott Kauffman
3104 Ryer Road East
Walnut Grove, CA 95690
(916) 775-1973

Midwest JRT Club
c/o Tandee Morris
39 West 348 Bolcum Rd.
St. Charles, IL 60175
(630) 443-0840

Oklahoma JRT Club
c/o Doug Minnich
1505 Oriole Dr.
Norman, OK 73072
(405) 321-4818

Pacific North West JRT Network
c/o Conni Martin
19525 NE 159th St.
Woodinville, WA 98072
(206) 885-9858

The South Pennsylvania JRT Club
c/o Wendy Wynne-Wilson
200 West Ridge Rd.
Dillsburg, PA 17019
(717) 432-9875

Southcoast JRT Club
c/o Don Tait
5013 Mindora Dr.
Torrance, CA 90505
(310) 543-4904

Southland JRTC Club
c/o Meredith Hindle-Rennie
2511 F Rd.
Loxahatchee, FL 33470
(561) 793-7888

Southwest JRT Network
c/o Joyce Cox
3159 Altman Dr.
Dallas, TX 75229
(214) 352-9649

Yankee JRT Network
c/o Joyce Robin
75 Pond St.
Seekonk, MA 02771
(508) 761-6684

The Jack Russell Terrier Club of America's Judges and Hunting Certificates

The Jack Russell Terrier Club of America has developed a structure of training and testing judges for aiding the education of those interested in working their dogs below ground. It is possible for JRTCA members to seek a judge for a day in the field to evaluate the working ability of a dog.

The club promotes a policy of catch and release. Dogs are used to finding animals below ground, but harm is not the intent of this relationship. The dog is used to baying at the animal in the earthen den. The animal is not harmed as any requirement for certificate work.

Exposing a pet to work is a serious responsibility. Only owners whose dogs are already working should seek the time of a judge, and those that want to learn from a judge should state so. The dog is kept on a leash and under the supervision of the judge. Most people who seek the time and company of a JRTCA working judge have a well-trained dog ready to be certified. Training sessions are not the time to seek certification of a working dog. Those seeking a training session should not request documentation of a successful hunt. The JRTCA Natural Hunting Certificate is a meaningful award given to a practiced working dog. The dog should be hunting successfully on a regular basis before approaching a judge to witness the dog at work for certification.

Only a JRTCA working judge can issue a certificate. This judge had to serve as a go-to-ground judge before fulfilling working judge requirements. Both go-to-ground judge and working judge applicants are required to hunt their own dogs for a period of two years before entering the program to become a judge. There is an apprentice program as well as required testing for JRTCA judges. All judges must be familiar with the wild animals in their area of the country and hold a small game license in their resident state. Full knowledge of the history and the Standard of the Jack Russell Terrier is expected of each judge.

To earn a Natural Hunting Certificate Below Ground, the terrier must enter a natural earth or rock den and locate the quarry on its own. The dog needs to disappear from sight into the earth. It must mark the animal below ground and bolt it, draw it or stay with it until it can be dug to. If it cannot be dug out, the judge must be absolutely sure that the dog reached its prize. The animal the dog meets must be identified by the judge.

Working dogs are evaluated by certified judges.

When there are other dogs used in the field, the terrier must work in such a manner that if it were the only dog there that day, locating the earth-dwelling resident would have been successful. Only one dog can earn a certificate to the quarry located. A second dog cannot be sent in after the first has located.

THE JACK RUSSELL TERRIER CLUB OF AMERICA'S ACHIEVEMENT CERTIFICATES

The Jack Russell Terrier Club of America awards five defined certificates of achievement to JRTCA-registered or recorded terriers. There are Trial, Natural Hunting, Sporting, Agility and Obedience certificates.

The Trial Certificate is awarded to a dog that has competed in a go-to-ground competition. The dog must first willingly enter an artificial earth made from a tunnel nine inches square, buried or bridging the ground and made to look like a natural burrow. The dog in the novice competition must go ten feet in the tunnel with one 90-degree turn. The dog has one minute to travel to a safely caged pair of rats behind smooth bars in a boxed area, with the judge observing and timing the competition. It may leave the tunnel several times but has only one minute to get to the rats. The dog is required to work, which consists of baying, barking or scratching. Even staring intently at the rats is considered acceptable. The dog must stay at work for thirty seconds.

The second stage is the Open Competition, in which the dog must travel thirty feet with two turns. It may exit the tunnel one time only. The dog must reach the caged rats in thirty seconds and work for a minute.

When it completes with both a successful time and quality of work in the Open Competition, the dog may apply for a Trial Certificate. This certificate is secured by sending the appropriate fee with a copy of the score sheet to the JRTCA. A Jack Russell must be registered or recorded with the JRTCA to be eligible for a Trial Certificate. If the terrier is not registered at the time of achieving 100 percent in the Open class, the owner may hold on to the score sheet and submit it with the application for the dog's registration. If the dog is accepted into the registry for the JRTCA, a Trial Certificate will be sent with its registration certificate.

The Trial Certificate is good for the life of the dog. The dog may then compete in the Certificate

Successful completion of a go-to-ground competition earns a JRT a Trial Certificate.

class at any JRTCA Competition. The dog may never compete in the Novice or Open classes again. Puppies and adults have their own divisions in the competition. The Championship Certificate classes are often divided into two size categories: from ten- to twelve-and-one-half-inch dogs and those that are over twelve-and-one-half inches and up to fifteen inches.

The dogs enjoy the competition immensely. It is a race below ground and a test of the dog's natural instincts as a locator. The competition provides a chance for dogs that are not used in field hunting to enjoy themselves in a safe simulated hunting situation. It shows the gameness of a dog and encourages a partnership between dog and handler. It never indicates an experienced earth worker and is more of a game to the dog. True work must be proven in a natural situation.

As a judge of such competitions, I wish to assure the reader the laboratory rats are well cared for by the judge and always treated humanely. They are provided with food and water. Often they sleep through the competition and need to be awakened to be of interest to the dogs that evaluate the rats upon reaching them. The intelligent terrier quickly discovers that it will not be able to reach the rats and may find the game uninteresting. Many JRTs put their heart and soul into trying to solve the puzzle and remove the barriers, sounding loudly and being active the entire time. The barrier is safe for both the dogs and the rats.

THE SPORTING CERTIFICATE

The JRTCA Sporting Certificate is awarded to both Jack Russells that have worked unformidable quarry such as rats, squirrel, mice, etc., and those working traditional quarry in man-made earth such as stone, walls, drains or hay lofts. It is issued to dogs that have been hunted regularly for at least a year. It is hoped that earning this certificate will encourage people to get out in the field with their terriers and serve as a precursor to earning a JRTCA Natural Hunting Certificate. Earning a Sporting Certificate will not make a terrier eligible for the Working Terrier classes at JRTCA-sanctioned trials or affect their status in the Go-to-Ground division.

The following criteria must be met before a JRTCA Sporting Certificate is issued:

1. A written, detailed report describing the dog's hunting experience, along with a filing fee, must be sent to the JRTCA Club Office. The report must be signed by the owner and one other JRTCA member that has witnessed the dog hunting on at least four occasions and acknowledges its use for regular hunting. The witness need not be a JRTCA working judge.

2. The terrier must work solely on its own to locate, work and dispatch (or bolt) the quarry.

3. There is to be no hunting or working the same quarry over and over with different terriers.

4. The owner of the Jack Russell must be a member of the JRTCA in good standing, and the terrier must be registered or recorded with the JRTCA.

5. Photographs of the terrier's work are suggested, but not mandatory.

THE JACK RUSSELL TERRIER CLUB OF AMERICA'S NATURAL HUNTING CERTIFICATE BELOW GROUND IN THE FIELD

The JRTCA Natural Hunting Certificate Below Ground in the Field is the highest certificate awarded by the JRTCA to a proven working Jack Russell. It is awarded by a sanctioned working judge that witnesses the work of the dog and handler. The dog must be registered or recorded with the JRTCA. The dog and owner must work together as a combined team to be awarded this certificate. A certificate may be awarded several times to the same dog, as long as each time it is earned for different successful work below ground meeting formidable approved earth dwellers.

The dog may qualify by having the creature it locates leave by choice through an exit tunnel and come to the surface. Qualifying work includes baying or barking, which holds the position of the animal encountered with the influence of the dog's presence until it is dug to and released unharmed. If the dog is called out, it must be determined by the judge and handler that the dog reached the resident of the tunnel and without question identified it. There are instances where the dog may have direct contact and draw. Safe release of any encountered earth dweller is favored. The dog is not required or requested to inflict any harm.

Certificate work is reserved for dogs and handlers that are experienced working as a team. The dog must be proven before being awarded a certificate. The JRTCA awards the JRTCA Bronze Medallion for Special Merit in the Field. When a dog is a successful locator and worker earning three or more Natural Hunting Certificates, it qualifies for this special honor. Working is a strong characteristic and part of the history of the breed, and it is encouraged to preserve the breed as it has been for hundreds of years.

A P P E N D I X   E

Resources

BIBLIOGRAPHY

Benjamin, Carol Lea. *Surviving Your Dog's Adolescence.* New York: Howell Book House, 1993.

Brown, Catherine Romaine. *The Jack Russell Terrier: An Owner's Guide to a Happy, Healthy Pet.* New York: Howell Book House, 1996.

Carlson, Delbert G., DVM, and James M. Giffin, MD. *Dog Owner's Home Veterinary Handbook.* New York: Howell Book House, 1992.

Chapman, Eddie. *The Working Jack Russell Terrier.* Dorchester, Dorset, England: The Dorset Press, 1985.

DiBittetto, James, DVM, and Sarah Hodgson. *You and Your Puppy.* New York: Howell Book House, 1995.

Fisher, John. *Why Does My Dog…?* New York: Howell Book House, 1991.

Gilbert, Edward M. Jr., and Thelma R. Brown. *K-9 Structure & Terminology.* New York: Howell Book House, 1995.

Harcombe, David. *Every Man's Hand*. Great Britain: WBC Limited, 1992.

Hobson, J. C. Jeremy. *Working Terriers*. New York: Howell Book House, 1989.

James, Kenneth. *Working Jack Russell Terriers*. Bedford, PA: Hunter House Press, 1995.

Kalstone, Shirlee. *How to Housebreak Your Dog in 7 Days*. New York: Bantam Books, 1985.

Lent, Pat Adams. *Sport with Terriers*. Rome, NY: Arner Publications, 1973.

Lyon, McDowell. *The Dog in Action*. New York, NY: Howell Book House, 1978.

Massey, Marilyn. *Above and Below Ground: The Jack Russell Terrier in North America*. Virginia: Woodluck Publications, 1985.

Rafe, Stephen C. *Your New Baby & Bowser*. Fairfax, VA: Denlingers Publications, Ltd., 1990.

Robinson, Roy. *Genetics for Dog Breeders*. Oxford, England: Pergamon Press plc, 1990.

Schnieper, Claudia. *On the Trail of the Fox*. Lucerne, Switzerland: Kinderbuchverlag, 1985.

Seranne, Ann. *The Joy of Breeding Your Own Show Dog*. New York: Howell Book House, 1995.

Serpell, James (Editor). *The Domestic Dog*. Cambridge, England: Cambridge University Press, 1995.

Sparrow, Geoffrey. *The Terrier's Vocation*. London: J. A. Allen & Co., 1949.

Syrotuck, William G. *Scent and the Scenting Dog*. Rome, NY: Arner Publications, 1972.

Volhard, Jack, and Melissa Bartlett. *What All Good Dogs Should Know: The Sensible Way to Train*. New York: Howell Book House, 1991.

Willis, Malcolm B. *Genetics of the Dog*. New York: Howell Book House, 1989.

NATIONAL BREED CLUB

The Jack Russell Terrier Club of America
P.O. Box 4527
Lutherville, MD 21094-4527

The club can provide you with information on all aspects of the breed, as well as the Russell Rescue contact nearest you. Inquire about membership.

MAGAZINE

True Grit
The Official Publication of the Jack Russell Terrier Club of America
P.O. Box 4527
Lutherville, MD 21094-4527

Index